TROY

AND THE TROJANS

TROY

AND THE TROJANS

Carl W. Blegen

**BARNES
&NOBLE**
BOOKS
NEW YORK

This edition published by Barnes & Noble, Inc.,
by arrangement with Thames & Hudson, Inc.

1995 Barnes & Noble Books

ISBN 1-56619-823-2

Printed and bound in the United States of America

M 9 8 7 6 5 4 3 2 1

CONTENTS

LIST OF ILLUSTRATIONS 6

ACKNOWLEDGMENTS 11

I TROY OF THE HOMERIC
POEMS 13

II THE ARCHAEOLOGICAL TROY 21

III THE EARLY BRONZE AGE: TROY I 39

IV THE EARLY BRONZE AGE: TROY II 59

V THE EARLY BRONZE AGE:
TROY III TO V 91

    Troy III 91

    Troy IV 99

    Troy V 105

VI THE MIDDLE AND LATE BRONZE
AGE: TROY VI 111

VII TROY VII*a* 147

VIII TROY VII*b* 165

    Troy VIIb 1 165

    Troy VIIb 2 167

CHRONOLOGY 173

SELECTED BIBLIOGRAPHY 175

NOTES ON THE PLATES 177

INDEX 185

Plates follow page 110

ILLUSTRATIONS

PLATES

1 The mound of Troy (1935) from north
2 The mound of Troy (1937) from east
3 Balli Dagh rising above the Scamander
4 W. T. Semple, W. Dörpfeld, Mrs Semple at Troy
5, 6 Pinnacles left by Schliemann
7 Schliemann's North-South Trench in 1938
8 Fortification wall and tower flanking South Gate, Troy I
9 South face of tower and wall beyond, Troy I
10 Fortification walls, late Troy I and Troy II
11 Wall of Early Troy I in herringbone style
12 House of Phase Ia beneath a house of Ib
13 House of Phase Ib
14 Infant burial in pottery jar
15 Miscellaneous objects of Troy I
16 Human faces incised on rims of bowls, and tubular lugs, Troy I
17 Sculptured stele of Troy I
18 Burial of child, Troy I
19 Fortification wall of Troy II
20 Stone column base of Phase IIc
21 Great ramp ascending to Gate FM, Troy II
22 Room with pots lying on floor, Phase IIg
23 Gold sauceboat from Schliemann's 'Great Treasure'

PLATES 24 Gold diadem from Schliemann's 'Great Treasure'

25 Royal battle-axes from Schliemann's 'Treasure L'

26 Miscellaneous objects of Troy II

27 Pots of Troy II

28 Child burial beneath floor, Phase IIg

29 House walls of Troy III

30 Miscellaneous objects of Troy III

31 Face pots and face lids of Troy III

32 Some pots of Troy IV

33 Miscellaneous objects of Troy IV

34 Hearth and cooking stand, Phase Vb

35 Plastered walls and corner seat, Phase Vb

36 Miscellaneous objects of Troy V

37 Fragments of face pots, red-cross bowls and decorative handles, Troy V

38 Tower and east fortification wall, Troy VI

39 Northeast Tower VI g

40 Tower VI g in 1893

41 Section of east fortification wall in 1894

42 Entrance through East Gate (VI S)

43 Fortification wall of Troy VI: angle of wall with Tower VI k

44 Sections of east fortification wall in 1894

45 Tower VI i, south wall and pillars

46 Fortification wall of Troy VI, Section 4

47 South Gate (VI T) in 1937

48 Fortification wall of Troy VI, Section 6

49 House VI G

7

PLATES 50 Pillar House

51 Miscellaneous objects of Troy VI

52 Wall of House VI E, fortification wall and earthquake debris

53 House VI F, from southwest

54 House VI F, offset in masonry

55 Western corner of House VI M in 1893

56 Mycenaean and Grey Minyan pots from Troy VI

57 Handles in form of animal heads, Troy VI

58 Burial urns in cremation cemetery, Late Troy VI

59 Fallen stones from fortification wall of Troy VI

60 Houses of Troy VII

61 House VII gamma of Period VIIa

62 Small houses of Troy VII

63 House VII theta of Troy VIIa

64 Miscellaneous objects of Troy VIIa

65 Wall of Troy VIIb, with orthostates

66 Miscellaneous objects of Troy VIIb

67 Knobbed Ware: characteristic pots

FIGURES 1 *Map of the Troad, p. 22*

2 *Plan of Troy, p. 29*

3 *Stratification in South part of mound, pp. 30–1*

4 *Cross-section of mound, p. 32*

5, 6 *Diagrammatic sections through pinnacle, pp. 33, 34*

7 *Diagrammatic section of deposit Troy I, pp. 42–3*

FIGURES   *8*   *Plan: fortification and houses, Troy I, p. 45*

9   *Decorated whorls, Troy I, p. 50*

10   *Stone hammer-axe, Troy I, p. 51*

11   *Characteristic pottery shapes, Troy I, p. 52*

12   *Pots with incised decoration, Troy I, p. 53*

13   *Incised patterns on bowl rims, Troy I, p. 54*

14   *Faces on rim projections of bowls, p. 55*

15   *Plan of citadel in Phase IIc, p. 65*

16   *Decorated whorls, Troy II, p. 72*

17   *Plan of house complex, Phase IIg, p. 73*

18   *Gold pin, Phase IIg, p. 74*

19   *Characteristic pottery shapes, Troy II, p. 80*

20   *Plan of houses, Troy III, p. 93*

21   *Decorated whorls, Troy III, p. 95*

22   *Characteristic pottery shapes, Troy III, p. 96*

23   *Lids decorated with human faces,*
     Troy III, p. 98

24   *Plan of houses, Phase IVa, p. 101*

25   *Decorated whorls, Troy IV, p. 103*

26   *Characteristic pottery shapes, Troy IV, p. 104*

27   *Plan of houses, Troy Vb, p. 106*

28   *Decorated whorls, Troy V, p. 108*

29   *Characteristic pottery shapes, Troy V, p. 109*

30   *Characteristic shapes of Grey Minyan Ware,*
     Troy VI, p. 114

31   *Plan of fortification and buildings, Troy VI, p. 115*

32   *Plan of gates, Pillar House and House 630,*
     p. 118

33   *Plan of House 630, Early VI, p. 125*

FIGURES *34*   *Plan of eastern side of citadel, Troy VI, p.* 128

35   *Plan of House VI F, p.* 135

36   *Diagrammatic plan of buildings, Troy VII, p.* 148

37   *Plan of houses, Troy VIIa, p.* 151

38   *Plan of Houses 730 and 731, Troy VIIa, p.* 155

39   *Characteristic pottery shapes, Troy VIIa, p.* 157

40   *Mycenaean Ware, Troy VIIa, p.* 158

41   *Plan of buildings, Troy VIIb, p.* 166

42   *Characteristic shapes of Knobbed Ware, Troy VIIb, p.* 170

Acknowledgments

I<small>T HAS BEEN</small> a pleasant task, though filled with nostalgic memories, to turn back – almost a quarter of a century after the close of the Cincinnati excavations at Troy – in an attempt to write a brief general survey dealing with the work done at that site since 1870 and with what it has yielded. Professor Semple keenly desired that such a book should be produced, and I undertook to try to prepare it.

At the outset in fulfilling this commitment I would like to acknowledge my great debt to our famous predecessors, Heinrich Schliemann and Wilhelm Dörpfeld, who discovered and uncovered most of the important Trojan monuments.

Even more I owe to William T. Semple and Louise Semple who founded the Cincinnati Archaeological Expedition, made its work possible, and gave me the opportunity of directing operations in the field.

I am also under deep obligation to all my colleagues in the seven seasons from 1932 to 1938 who assisted not only in supervising digging, but in studying and interpreting what was found. Marion Rawson and John L. Caskey deserve special mention.

I would likewise recall the generosity of the German Archaeological Institute in relinquishing rights to the site in our favour, and in providing a grant to enable Dr F. W. Goethert to join the staff at Troy. As Director of the Branch of the German Archaeological Institute in Istanbul Dr K. Bittel, now President of that Institute, often visited us at Troy and taught us much that was invaluable. Dr Bittel and Professor Goethert have further aided me in obtaining photographs.

It is a pleasure also to thank the Turkish archaeological officials who always cordially helped us when we were in difficulties and showed us unfailing courtesies, especially my friend Hamit Zübeyr Košay, Director of the Turkish Arch-aeological Service at the time of our excavations. I wish also to remember the late Aziz Ogan, Director of the Archaeological Museum in Istanbul, and the late Remzi Oğuz Arik who worked with us as Commissioner in 1935 and 1936.

Elizabeth Blegen has patiently read or listened to the text of the book and has made many constructive suggestions. Marion Rawson scrutinised the manuscript with a keen eye and has saved me from innumerable errors and lapses; and to her I am immeasurably indebted for the selection and procure-ment of most of the illustrations as well as for the arrangement of many plates.

Princeton University Press and its Director, Herbert Bailey, have generously cooperated in waiving reservations on free use of material from the four volumes of *Troy*, the final report of the Cincinnati Expedition.

The photographs reproduced in Plates 11, 19, 40, 41, 44 and 55 are from negatives belonging to the German Arch-aeological Institute in Athens to which I am greatly beholden. Plates 23, 24 and 25 I owe to the Museum für Vor- und Früh-Geschichte in Berlin. All the other Plates are made from photographs taken at Troy by members of the Cincinnati Expedition, and most of them have been published in the several volumes of *Troy*.

Miss Hero Athanasiades has substantially aided me with drawings and sketches: for Figure 4 borrowed from Dörpfeld's *Troja und Ilion,* and for Figures 2, 3, 5–31, 33–35, 39, 40 and 42, all adapted from *Troy* I to IV. To William B. Dins-moor, Jr, I am indebted for the adaptations from the *Troy* volumes that appear in Figures 32, 36, 37, 38 and 41. I am also grateful to H. A. Shelley, who redrew Fig. 1 from an original kindly provided by Charles Williams.

C.W.B.

CHAPTER I

Troy of the Homeric Poems

IN THE ILIAD and the *Odyssey* Troy appears as a great widespread city, defended by mighty walls and towers. The fortress enclosed an area extensive enough to provide room not only for its own large population, but also for the numerous allies who assembled to help repel the Achaean aggression and who found place for their chariots and horses and all other equipment. Some scholars have calculated that, as envisaged in the poems, more than 50,000 people could be accommodated. The city had wide streets, and an open *agora*, or square, was laid out in the upper part of the citadel, outside the 'splendid' palace of King Priam.

This building itself was of huge size: in addition to the halls of state, provided with porticoes built of well-fitted hewn stones, and the king's private apartments (*megara*, not described in detail), it contained 50 chambers, with walls of smoothly worked blocks, where Priam's sons lived with their wedded wives. There were, moreover, apparently beyond a court, 12 further rooms – built of well-dressed stone and roofed – for the king's daughters and their husbands. Other palaces, too, stood close at hand, among them the many-roomed abode (*domoi*) of Hector, a 'comfortable place to live in' with its spacious halls, or *megara*. Near-by stood the beautiful home in which Alexander, or Paris, lived with the lovely Helen. He himself had built it, employing the very best builders and craftsmen to be found in Troy, and its *thalamos*, perhaps Helen's own chamber, hall and court are duly mentioned. In the '*megaron*' Helen used to work at her weaving on a great loom. Yet another palatial house of several rooms (*domata*) was that of Priam's son Deiphobos, who after Alexander's death had married Helen. When the Achaean champions emerged from the wooden horse and captured Troy, Odysseus with Menelaus proceeded straight to that house and after a desperate struggle slew Deiphobos and recovered Helen, the beautiful.

Some of the public buildings, too, are recorded. One was the temple of Athena standing in the upper part of the city. In it was a cult image of the goddess, evidently seated, on the knees of which Hecuba and the elderly women of Troy laid costly robes when they prayed to Athena to drive back the raging Diomedes. There was likewise a temple of Apollo in the 'holy Pergamos' high in the citadel. It contained a spacious and rich '*adyton*', or inner shrine, in which Leto and Artemis healed and restored the wounded Aeneas, and Apollo filled him with fresh courage. Somewhere in the city there may have been a council chamber; at any rate Hector speaks to elders and councillors, who presumably had a covered meeting-place of some kind.

The information gleaned from reading the Homeric poems gives little or no idea of the city plan. The fortification wall, too, is only sketchily pictured, though we learn that it is well constructed of regular building blocks. There were high towers at intervals, one called the 'Great Tower of Ilion' which apparently stood near or beside the 'Scaean Gate'. It was there that the assembled Trojan elders, eloquent as cicadas sitting on a tree, admired the beauty of Helen when she came out, took her seat beside Priam, her father-in-law, and identified for him some of the leading heroes who were conspicuous in the Achaean ranks: King Agamemnon, son of Atreus, Odysseus, clever and enterprising, and the mighty Ajax; but she looked in vain for her twin brothers, Castor and Pollux, not knowing that they had already met their fate and were buried in the soil of Lacedaemon.

It was to the Great Tower by the 'Scaean Gate' that Andromache, too, went with her infant son and his nurse; and there Hector found them and bade farewell when he returned to the battlefield. The regular way to and from the plain passed through this gate, and Priam drove through it in his chariot when he went out to see the duel between Paris and Menelaus. It was also here that evil fate caused Hector to remain alone outside the walls to face Achilles while all his Trojan comrades took refuge inside the battlements.

In the *Iliad* a 'Dardanian Gate' is three times mentioned, presumably having been so named because it opened on to the road that led to Dardania, far away toward the south on the slopes of Mt Ida 'with the many springs'. In one passage the goddess Hera is deriding the Achaeans as helpless without Achilles, for when he was taking part in the struggle the Trojans were frightened even to come out in front of the Dardanian Gate, but now that he was absent, they boldly ventured down to the ships themselves. It was the shelter of this same Dardanian Gate that Hector vainly sought to reach each time he passed it as he fled before his pursuer, Achilles, three times around the walls of Troy. And when Hector was slain and Achilles dragged the body in the dust behind his chariot, it was from the Dardanian Gate that Priam wished to go forth to plead for honourable treatment, and was with difficulty held back by his own people.

Troy evidently had other gates in addition to the two that bear specific names. In the second book of the *Iliad*, at any rate, when Hector, inspired by the messenger Iris, ordered the Trojans and their allies to draw up and lead out their entire forces in battle order, 'all the gates' were opened and the whole host poured out. This would imply that there were certainly more than two gates. The use of the plural form of the word *pylai* for a gate seems to be normal; that was undoubtedly because a gate was regularly fitted with double doors swinging, one to each side, on pivots.

We read that there were angles in the walls. Along one of them Patroclus three times attempted to climb to the top of the fortification only to be hurled back thrice by Apollo. Is this possibly a reference to the characteristic offsets so well known in the great wall of Troy VI and VIIa?

One of the odd things about the city is the fact that it bore two different names. In the *Iliad* and the *Odyssey* it is called, without apparent distinction, either Troy (*Troie*) or Ilios. Troy was perhaps originally the more general name, applying to the whole countryside – the Troad – while Ilios more specifically designated the actual city, but in the Homeric poems this distinction is not maintained, and either name is used without prejudice to mean the city. In the *Iliad* the name Ilios appears 106 times, more than twice as often as Troy, which occurs 50 times. In the *Odyssey* Troy has an advantage of nearly four to three over Ilios, appearing 25 times, while we meet the latter in 19 instances. In the classical period and later the regular name of the city that still survived on the site had become Ilion and the inhabitants were known as Ilians.

Although the Homeric poems, as we have seen, provide no systematic description of the city, some – if not much – authentic information is undoubtedly preserved in the distinctive adjectives that are frequently attached – in more or less often repeated phrases – to the one name or the other, Ilios or Troy. Associated with Ilios are eleven different adjectives or epithets, and with Troy there are ten. Only one term makes an identical appearance in both lists, namely, *euteicheos*, 'well-walled', which is applied alike both to Troy (twice) and to Ilios (four times). With that exception the epithets of one list are restricted exclusively to Ilios, and those of the other list just as rigidly to Troy, though they are in a good many instances similar in meaning.

Troy is a 'broad city', 'with wide streets'; it has 'lofty gates' and 'fine towers'; it is a 'great city', 'the city of Priam', 'the city of the Trojans', and it also possesses – in two similar adjectives – 'deep rich soil'.

Ilios is 'holy' and 'sacred'; 'steep', 'sheer', and 'frowning'; but a 'well-built' city, 'comfortable to live in', though 'very windy'; it is likewise 'lovely', and it 'has good foals'.

This latter idea is clearly reflected in the most common of all the 16 different adjectives used in the *Iliad* to characterise the Trojan people themselves: in 19 passages they are called *hippo-damoi*, 'tamers of horses'. Just as *eupolos*, 'having fine foals', is never said of any city other than Ilios, so *hippodamoi* is never applied in the epic to any entire people other than the Trojans, although the epithet *hippodamos* is conferred on nine individual heroes who were renowned for their horsemanship (Antenor, Atreus, Castor, Diomedes, Hector, Hippasos, Hyperenor, Thrasymedes, and Tydeus). The possession of good horses and the ability to tame them thus evidently came to be regarded as notable characteristics of the people of Troy.

Among the other qualifying adjectives and epithets more or less frequently employed in the *Iliad* in referring to the Trojans *megathymoi*, 'high-spirited', occurs in eleven instances, *hyper-thymoi*, with virtually the same meaning, in seven; *agerochoi*, 'lordly', appears five times, *hyperphialoi*, 'arrogant' or 'overween-ing' four, *agavoi*, 'illustrious', thrice, *megaletores*, 'great hearted' twice and, only once each, *agenores*, 'manly', *hyperenoreontes*, 'overbearing' and *hybristai*, 'insolent'. All nine of the foregoing epithets, occurring in an aggregate of 35 instances, are approxi-mately synonymous in meaning and they depict the Trojans as a proud, arrogant people.

The rest of the epithets applied in the *Iliad* to the Trojans are more general and conventional: 'shield-bearing', four times; 'armed with cuirass' and 'fond of war' three times each, 'bronze-clad', twice; 'spearmen', once. In another single instance they are called *euepheneis*, meaning 'rich' or 'prosperous'.

The individual heroes, Achaean as well as Trojan, who appear in the epics usually have accompanying descriptive adjectives. Many of these are general terms that may be applied to almost any warrior on either side in the struggle; but there are also not a few that are of restricted use, being applied only to particular persons. Each one is presumably founded on some specific distinctive character, trait, appearance, or act attributed to the individual concerned. King Priam, for example, evidently possessed a spear with a shaft of ash wood, from which he acquired the epithet *eummelies*, 'with good ashen spear'. In the *Iliad* this adjective is restricted to the Trojans, Priam himself and the son (or sons) of Panthous, and never applied to others. Achilles likewise wielded a spear of ash which is called *melie*, a word reserved exclusively for this one particular weapon. The same hero has a monopoly in the adjective *podarkes*, 'swift-footed', and *podas okus*, 'fleet of foot' is also (except in one instance in the *Odyssey*) his own. Hector, too, has attached to him distinguishing adjectives, *korythaiolos*, 'with gleaming helmet', and *chalkokorystes*, 'bronze-helmeted', which he shares with no other man. Alexander is six times described as 'the husband of Helen of the beautiful hair'. His brother Deiphobos is distinguished by his 'white shield'. Agamemnon, Odysseus, Patroclus, Ajax, Nestor, and other heroes are nearly all endowed in the epic poems with comparable epithets, each presumably bestowed as peculiarly applicable to its exclusive bearer.

The sum total of all these casual, scattered bits of information about Troy and the Trojans (and about the Achaeans) that may be gleaned from the Homeric poems falls considerably short of what one might desire. It is to a great extent of general and typical nature, such as any poet might freely imagine about any royal stronghold, king and people. On the other hand, as we have seen, there are a good many items of detailed and distinctive knowledge and memory that seem unlikely to have been independently invented by pure poetic fancy.

The brilliant achievements of several men of outstanding ability and genius have during the past generation profoundly affected the views that scholars must now take with reference to Homer and Homeric problems as well as to the history of the Late Bronze Age in the Aegean. Most spectacular perhaps was the discovery by Michael Ventris in June 1952, that the clay tablets from Knossos and Pylos, inscribed in the Linear B script, are documents written in an early form of Greek. The Hellenic language is thus shown to have been in use in a Mycenaean palace.

Martin Nilsson had in fact already long ago pointed out that almost all the great concentrations of Greek myths cluster about the palaces and the populous cities that flourished in the Mycenaean Age, and he had convincingly demonstrated that the origin of Greek mythology must go back to that era.

Meanwhile, Milman Parry, in a notable series of penetrating studies, had proved conclusively that the *Iliad* and the *Odyssey* in their composition are to a great extent constructed of numer- ous fixed formular phrases that were originally created by and for oral poetry; they were handed down through generation after generation of bards and singers in a conservative poetic tradition that maintained itself for ages before any of the texts were committed to writing.

Denys Page has recently carried the demonstration still fur- ther, showing, with cogent reasoning, that many of the linguis- tic features in the poems are actual survivals from the Achaean or Mycenaean dialect of Mycenaean times: the distinctive descriptive epithets and characterisations of places and men were formulated by minstrels who were on the spot and were themselves familiar with the scenes, the culture and the chief personages whose glories they celebrated; and who during and after the war recited and sang their songs in the palaces of princes who had participated in the expeditions. Professor Page has likewise marshalled all the archaeological evidence that bears on the history of the Mycenaean Age, the Trojan War, and on Homeric problems.

It can no longer be doubted, when one surveys the state of our knowledge today, that there really was an actual historical Trojan War in which a coalition of Achaeans, or Mycenaeans, under a king whose overlordship was recognised, fought against the people of Troy and their allies. The magnitude and the duration of the struggle may have been exaggerated by folk memory in later times, and the numbers of the participants have been very over-generously estimated in the epic poems. Many major as well as minor incidents were undoubtedly invented and introduced into the tale in its course through the centuries. But – as has been so ably established by Professor Page – the internal evidence of the *Iliad* itself, in the abundant structural and linguistic survivals it contains, is sufficient, even without the testimony of archaeology, to demonstrate not only that the tradition of the expedition against Troy must have a basis of historical fact, but furthermore that a good many of the indivi-dual heroes – though probably not all – who are mentioned in the poems were drawn from real personalities as they were observed by accompanying minstrels at the time of the events in which they played their parts.

CHAPTER II

The Archaeological Troy

THE ARCHAEOLOGICAL TROY – the Troy that was built by masons, carpenters and labourers, of rough stones or squared-building blocks, and crude bricks made with straw, of wooden timbers and beams, of clay and probably thatch for the roofing – that Troy, in its ruined state today, differs greatly, so far as its appearance is concerned, from the glamorous citadel pictured in the epic poems. But – if one is blessed with a little imagination – when one stands on the ancient hill top in the extreme northwestern corner of Asia Minor and looks out over the Trojan plain and thinks of some of the many exciting scenes it has witnessed, one cannot escape feeling that this Troy, too, has a powerful touch of enchantment.

Fig. 1

The ruins, called Hissarlik, occupy the western tip of a low ridge coming from the east and ending somewhat abruptly in steep slopes on the north and west and a more gradual descent toward the south. Some four miles distant to the westward, across the flat plain of the tree-bordered Scamander, and beyond a line of low hills, is the Aegean Sea. On it, to the southwest, floats the island of Tenedos – which was sacked by Achilles – and much farther northward is Imbros, where, the sorrowing Hecuba says, some of her sons who had been captured by Achilles were sold into slavery. Behind Imbros, on a clear day, one sees the twin-peaked height of Samothrace, and often when the weather is at its clearest, one can even make out the summit of Mount Athos. Looking on all this one remembers the story told by Aischylos of the fire-signals that flashed from peak to peak across the sea and land to Mycenae, announcing to Clytemnestra the news that Troy had been captured.

Plates 1, 2

To the north of Hissarlik and less than an hour's walk away is the Hellespont, the Straits now called the Dardanelles, with

Fig. 1 Sketch map of the Troad in northwest Asia Minor

the Gallipoli peninsula rising in the background, a region rich in historical associations from ancient to modern times. It was there, tradition asserts, that Protesilaos was buried, the first eager hero to leap ashore from his ship when the Achaean fleet drew near to the Trojan land. A conspicuous ancient tumulus is still called the Tomb of Protesilaos.

Because of the ruined walls that covered it, the end of the Trojan ridge was long known to the Turks as Hissarlik, or 'the fortress'. On the evidence of inscriptions discovered here it was identified more than 150 years ago as the site of Hellenistic and Roman Ilion. Until late in the nineteenth century many serious orthodox classical scholars, especially in Germany and on the Continent, believed and asserted that the Homeric poems were altogether products of free poetic imagination with no basis of reality, and that it would therefore be useless and foolish to look for an actual physical Troy. The romantic school, on the other hand, consisting chiefly of English, but with a good many German scholars, was convinced that Troy had really existed. Influenced by the grandeur of the city as depicted in the *Iliad*, nearly all of them thought the site could be recognised in a lofty stronghold called Balli Dagh, that rises steeply above the gorge through which the Scamander emerges from the hills into the lower plain. At the western foot of this cliff is the small village of Bunarbashi, notable for its copious springs. Excavations in a small way on the hill were undertaken by several explorers, in particular in 1864 by an Austrian, G. von Hahn; the evidence was interpreted by him as confirming the identification, and most of those who believed in a real Troy were content to accept this conclusion.

Plate 3

In 1822 Charles Maclaren had published in Edinburgh a book entitled *A Dissertation on the Topography of the Plain of Troy*, which received far less attention than it deserved. Maclaren, collecting all the topographical information that could be gleaned from the *Iliad*, and comparing it with the best procurable modern maps of the region, revived the view, which prevailed in antiquity from classical to Roman times, holding that Hellenistic and later Ilion occupied the same site as the Troy of Priam and Homer. Grote accepted this thesis which was favourably received by a good many others in England and by one or two German students of Homer.

Nearly half a century later Frank Calvert, who lived in the Troad and who owned part of the hill of Hissarlik, after much study and exploration came to the same conclusion. He was the first – in 1865 – to apply the test of actual digging to the spot. It was no more than a small sounding, but it brought to light Roman, Hellenistic, and prehistoric pottery and other remains. Calvert showed the site to Schliemann, who in 1868 visited the Troad and who had looked at Balli Dagh, but found it unsatisfactory as the site of Priam's Troy. With great enthusiasm Schliemann accepted as preferable the identification of the mound at Hissarlik and resolved to excavate it on a grand scale. In 1870 he was ready to begin his long series of campaigns that were continued from time to time until 1890. To Heinrich Schliemann must be awarded full credit for the discovery, for establishing its validity, and for arousing immense interest in Homer and archaeology not only on the part of classical students but of the educated world and of the general public.

The mound of Hissarlik had a maximum length of some 200 m. and was less than 150 m. wide. It rose approximately 31.20 m. above the level of the plain at its northern foot, the summit, composed of debris of human habitation, reaching an elevation of about 38.50 m. above sea-level. For an administrative centre and a capital the situation was admirably suited, both for security and for economic reasons. It lay near enough to the sea to have landing places and perhaps a small port or two within easy reach, and yet far enough away to be reasonably safe from sudden hostile attacks or piratical raids. It also controlled a land route that apparently came up along the western coastal region of Asia Minor to the shortest crossing of the straits from Asia to Europe. From its vantage grounds it could no doubt likewise dominate traffic up and down the straits, and perhaps tolls of some kind were exacted from those who passed.

Few comparable ancient sites have been so extensively and so searchingly excavated as Hissarlik. After Calvert's initial scratching of the surface in 1865, Schliemann carried out seven major campaigns of digging, besides several minor operations, between 1870 and 1890, usually employing upwards of 100, sometimes more than 150, workmen, and often continuing through a season of four months and longer. The hours of work ran from sunrise to sunset, and an immense volume of earth and stones was dug up and moved away. After Schliemann's death in late December 1890, his colleague and successor, Professor Wilhelm Dörpfeld, operating on a large scale, resumed the undertaking in two additional campaigns in 1893 and 1894. More than a generation was then allowed to pass without further work at Hissarlik; but in 1932 the Archaeological Expedition of the University of Cincinnati, under the general direction of Professor W. T. Semple, began a fresh investigation of the stratification and other problems, which was continued annually through seven seasons of three to four months each until 1938. After all these long-extended operations it is no wonder that the greater part of the mound has now been dug away altogether – most of it by Schliemann – and only one or two small pinnacles are left which still preserve the sequence of the superposed strata that made up the great mound before digging began.

Plate 4

Plates 5, 6

Schliemann's name is inseparably linked to this archaeological Troy which he has endowed with enduring romance. With his unshakeable faith in Homer, his boundless energy and enthusiasm, his organising ability, his resolute determination, and his unfailing persistence – all backed by abundant financial resources, which he had acquired by his own efforts – with all these qualifications, Schliemann overcame innumerable obstacles and difficulties and achieved a brilliant success: he compelled the professional archaeologists and classical scholars, many of them against their will, to give serious attention to his work, and he won world-wide fame for himself. The story of his rise by sheer, indomitable, intelligent industry from utter poverty in his youth to affluence and independence in his middle age, as told in a somewhat romantic autobiographical sketch which he published in an introduction to his large work *Ilios the City and Country of the Trojans*, will always have fascinated readers.

Schliemann left a vast collection of diaries, notebooks, papers, and correspondence, and several popular biographies have been issued; but there is still need for a better one. It seems to me that his ruling motives have been misinterpreted or at least distorted by some writers who think his driving force was a passion for gold, and they have laid undue emphasis on this – imagined – overpowering desire for gold and its effect on the course of his life. In his business career, it is true, Schliemann set out deliberately and unswervingly to amass a fortune. But once this was accomplished and he had embarked on his archaeological career, it was – as he often makes clear – not material treasure that he was primarily seeking: like most serious archaeologists, he had no real objection to finding gold, but the supreme dedicated aim of all his digging was to recover convincing evidence of the historic reality of the Trojan War and of the Homeric story of it – evidence, that is, that would convince the doubters and those who had no faith in the truth of Homer's account.

Much has been said, too, in condemnation of Schliemann's methods of excavation and of the many mistakes with which he has often been charged. Although there were some regrettable blunders, those criticisms are largely coloured by a comparison with modern techniques of digging; but it is only fair to remember that before 1876 very few persons, if anyone, yet really knew how excavations should properly be conducted. There was no science of archaeological investigation, and there was probably no other digger who was better than Schliemann in actual field work. In its early days excavation was little more than a high-class looting expedition to discover and to acquire interesting objects to be carried away for exhibition in a museum. Little attention was paid to the context in which anything was found. The observation and study of stratigraphy were scarcely known. Though not unmindful of the value of handsome and exciting objects to demonstrate the importance of his undertaking, Schliemann had a deeper purpose: he was seeking historical information. From his own mistakes he himself learned – and he was very quick at learning. He was a pioneer, and all those who have come after him have profited from his experience. By the end of his career he had made himself an experienced, trained, observant excavator who could hold his own with anyone; and he had the good sense to surround himself with a competent staff of assistants and colleagues.

Even without them, when, with the help only of his young wife, he discovered and cleared the royal shaft graves at Mycenae with their hundreds of small delicate objects, he did a remark-ably good piece of work; and, as Professor G. Karo says: 'No one who knows how to dig can fail to accord to Schliemann the highest recognition for his achievement.'

Schliemann was also gratifyingly prompt in publishing an account of what he had done. At the outset these reports (little more than excerpts from his day-book) were couched in simple language, perhaps somewhat naïve, but from the beginning they showed his power of objective observation and his faith-fulness in writing down in his day-books what he saw. The glory of discovering Troy and making it known to the world is his, and his fame was fairly won.

The accumulation of debris that formed the mound of Hissarlik before the excavations began was soon found by Schliemann to be enormously deep – more than 15 m. Since he started with the assumption – gained from Homer – that

Plate 7

the Troy of Priam was the original establishment on the hill, he thought its ruins must lie at the bottom of the vast deposit. Schliemann therefore resolved to cut a huge trench, some 40 m. wide, straight across the middle of the mound from north to south and to clear away everything in that area that was superposed above the lowest stratum. With the forces available in the 1870's it was a stupendous undertaking, offering a problem that would challenge even a modern expedition, provided with the latest improved equipment; and in carrying it out Schliemann ultimately judged it wise to reduce sub-stantially the scope of the project.

As he proceeded, he began to notice that the debris did not form a single homogeneous mass but had grown up by gradual accumulation in numerous superposed layers, one above the other, and evidently representing a like number of chronolog-ical stages or periods. In due course, Schliemann was able to distinguish at least seven, and ultimately, with Dörpfeld's aid, nine, main layers extending through the mound. He called them 'cities': First City, Second City, Third City, and so on, counting from the bottom upwards. Seeing that the lowest layer, Troy I, produced for the most part only rude stone and bone implements, primitive pottery, and very little metal – chiefly copper – he concluded that he had erred in thinking the First City to be the Troy of Homer, and he shifted his identification to a thick burned layer which he counted as the third from the bottom. In this deposit he discerned remains of a much higher culture, finding many 'treasures' of gold, silver, and copper or bronze, including one splendid hoard of royal weapons, vessels, and ornaments. In 1882 a further revision was made when Dörpfeld pointed out to Schliemann that the 'Burnt City' actually represented what must have been the final phase of Troy II. Some years later, in 1890, Schliemann and Dörpfeld together discovered that yet another modification was necessary; for near the southern border of the mound, far out-

Fig. 2

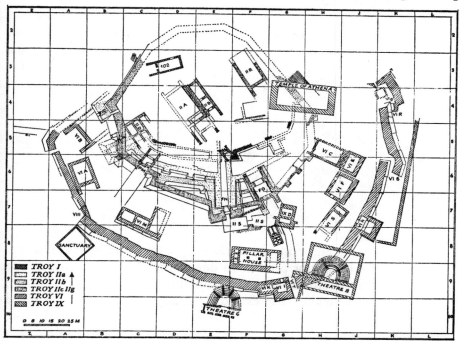

Fig. 2 Plan of Troy

side the fortification walls of Troy II, they came upon a large building (later called VI A) similar in plan to the throne-hall in the palaces at Mycenae and Tiryns; it was clearly associated with a deposit of Troy VI which contained a good many fragments of Mycenaean pottery of the types that were well known to the two excavators from their explorations at Mycenae and Tiryns. This was a startling blow to Schliemann, but he at once laid plans for a renewal of the excavations in a campaign on a large scale in 1891. Untimely death on the 26th of December 1890 deprived him of the opportunity to test by further digging whether it was necessary to shift Homer's Troy from the Second to the Sixth City.

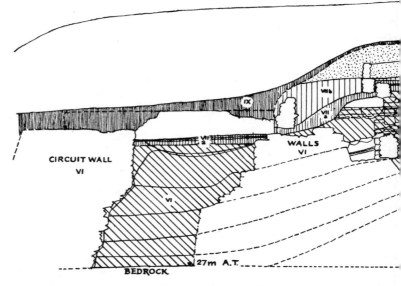

Fig. 3 Diagrammatic section of deposit in south part of mound

That privilege and task devolved upon Dörpfeld, who in 1893 and 1894 discovered the fortification walls and the great houses of Troy VI, in association with which he found much Mycenaean pottery. It therefore became clear that the Sixth Settlement must be, in part at least, contemporary with the strongholds of Tiryns and Mycenae, and Dörpfeld with confidence identified it as the Troy of Homer and Priam.

In its work some 40 years later the Archaeological Expedition of the University of Cincinnati was able to differentiate in *Figs. 3, 4, 5, 6* the undisturbed debris that was still left on the mound no fewer than 46 strata: each of the nine major layers, as had earlier been noted, was composed of two, three, five, eight, or even more minor strata, these subdivisions no doubt indicating lesser chronological phases within the main periods.

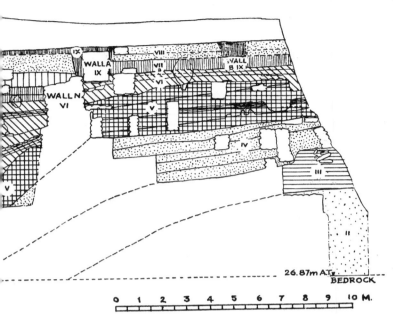

In broader terms, comparable with the system of Minoan classification and chronology introduced by Sir Arthur Evans, it has now become clear that the layers and periods from Troy I to and including Troy V belong to an era that corresponds to the Early Aegean Bronze Age, while the beginning of Troy VI marks the sharp turn to the Middle Bronze Age. The Sixth Settlement maintained itself without a real break into the later part of the Aegean Late Bronze Age, though the actual end of that era is represented by Troy VIIa and VIIb 1. These two phases, as Dörpfeld himself in 1937 suggested, might logically have been named Troy VIi and VIj, since they form a direct continuation of that culture; but it was feared that much confusion might be caused to scholars and readers accustomed to the hitherto prevailing terminology. With Troy VIIb 2, in

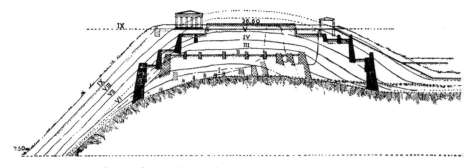

Fig. 4 Cross-section of mound from north to south

any event, we come to an abrupt change, apparently signalling the arrival of a new people. Exactly how long this régime survived is not yet known; but the site seems ultimately to have been abandoned and left deserted for some centuries until reoccupied about 700 BC by Hellenic colonists. The corresponding layer is called Troy VIII; and Troy IX then designates the period and ruins of the Hellenistic and Roman city of Ilion.

Visitors at excavations have often asked how it was possible for public buildings and private houses to be covered over so deeply by the heaping up of earth and debris. The enormous depth of the accumulation on the mound of Hissarlik might perhaps require a few words of explanation.

Throughout the Bronze Age nearly all ordinary dwellings were built with walls of crude brick which had generally been laid, within a sturdy framework of wood, on a low stone foundation, or socle, that projected a foot or more above ground. The roof was made of rough timbers or trunks of small trees, laid close together, supporting a thick layer of earth or clay probably topped by thatch. Because wood and thatch were freely used, fires were frequent in those times. When a building burned down the roof fell in and the walls collapsed; and the same was likely to happen if the roof was blown off by a gale. If rain followed, the unbaked brick dissolved into clay. In a closely packed village when one house caught fire it seems often to have spread across and wrecked the whole community. Unless this was the work of enemies the inhabitants generally survived, and at once set about rebuilding their homes. Bull-dozers and grading machines not being available, no attempt was made to clear away the wreckage; it was much easier and simpler to level out the debris, raising the original ground level considerably, burying the ruins, and then building the new house over them. This process was followed often at Troy and on each occasion the ground level rose two or three feet.

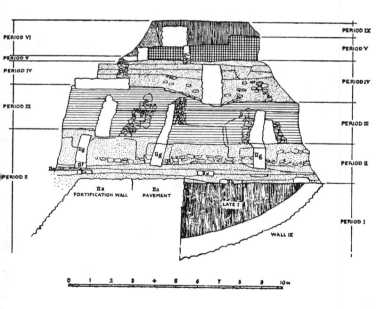

Fig. 5 Diagrammatic section B-B through pinnacle in Square E 6. As seen from southeast

33

There were other ways, too, in which appreciable contribu
tions to the steady growth of the mound were provided. Except
in palaces or luxurious mansions, floors were almost always
made of earth or clay stamped or trodden hard. There was no
provision for the disposal of rubbish and waste, no regular
collection of kitchen refuse. Everything discarded – bones,
unwanted food, broken dishes – was dropped on the floor
indoors or thrown out through the doorway into the street.

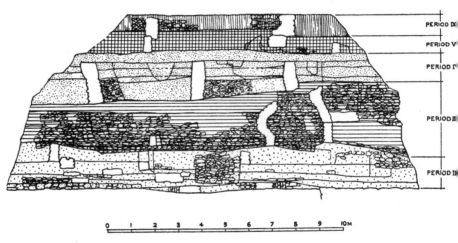

Fig. 6 Diagrammatic section A-A through pinnacle in Square E 6. As seen from southwest

Sooner or later there must have come a time when the floor
became so filled with animal bones and litter that even the
least squeamish household felt that something had to be done
in the way of a thorough spring cleaning. It was normally
accomplished in a practical, effective way: not by sweeping out
the offensive accumulation on the floor, but by bringing in a
good supply of fresh clean clay and spreading it out thickly to

cover the noxious deposit. In many a house, as demonstrated by the clearly marked stratification, this process was repeated time after time until the level of the floor rose so high that it was necessary to raise the roof and to rebuild the doorway. In one house of Troy III at least a dozen successive floors of this kind accounted for a rise of some three feet in the ground level.

It might be added parenthetically that archaeologists always prefer – in their field work – to meet with housekeeping of this careless type; for every accumulation that was covered over by a new clay floor is likely to contain many objects of various categories that were sealed up together, so to speak, in a closed deposit, and a sequence of such strata allows a study of develop‑ ment and progress within a period. On the other hand, tidy housekeeping, as exemplified in some houses of Troy V, has undoubtedly deprived modern excavators of untold treasures.

In dealing with Troy of the Bronze Age we encounter a great difficulty which perhaps ought to be pointed out before we turn to a survey of the physical remains of the many successive settlements. From the beginning of the First Settle‑ ment to the end of Troy VIIb 2 we have no contemporary written records to throw light on the history, religion, social organisation, economic life, and other aspects of Trojan culture. In Mesopotamia and Syria vast numbers of clay tablets, bearing records in various languages in the cuneiform script and others, have given abundant information on details of life in all its many facets. In Egypt, too, a multitude of documents on stone or papyrus has come to the aid of the archaeologist and his‑ torian. In Crete and Greece also clay tablets have been brought to light, one kind written in a script called Linear B in an early form of the Greek language, as demonstrated by Michael Ventris. When they have been fully interpreted they will help much toward an understanding of the bureaucratic form of administration and the economic system of the Mycenaean world. But at Troy not a single document has been found.

This does not necessarily mean that writing was unknown: records may have been kept on wood or on other perishable material which has vanished without leaving a trace; or, if inscribed on tablets of unbaked clay, the latter may not have had the fortune to be accidentally baked and preserved in an otherwise destructive fire, as happened at Knossos and Pylos.

Without written documents, in any event, the only source of information available in an attempt to reconstruct the history and manner of life of the Trojan people is the material brought to light by the excavations, the ruins of the walls and buildings of the successive settlements, and all the various and sundry objects recovered from the sequence of layers in the debris. Difficulties present themselves here, too; for exact records from the early campaigns, when most of the digging was done, are scanty and incomplete. The pottery and other objects of Troy I could for the most part be recognised; but in his *Catalogue of the Schliemann Collection*, Hubert Schmidt was unable to differentiate with certainty the pottery and most of the other material from the layers of Troy II, III, IV, and V, all of which had to be lumped together as an enormously large group representing a long era.

After Dörpfeld's excavations of 1893 and 1894 the character of Troy VI stood out clearly, and its general contemporaneity with Mycenae and Tiryns was fixed, though relatively little had survived to represent its achievements in art. Nor had the several phases of Troy VIIa, VIIb 1, and VIIb 2 been fully distinguished.

In the absence of written records, there is thus at Troy for all periods preceding the Eighth Settlement a total lack of independent evidence for dating the successive layers and strata with any sort of precision. The formidable depth of the deposit and the great number of the principal divisions and their many component subdivisions must inevitably be interpreted as pointing to a long chronology, but they do not tell how long;

and there are no fixed dates that stand by themselves. The only course left to us is to compare the objects found at Troy with those from other places, which have an established chronology of their own, and with which there might have been commercial or other connections. At almost all sites imported objects are occasionally found and there was evidently, in some instances, at least a mutual exchange of goods. In such circumstances synchronisms between the two regions may be validly established, but only if the exact findspot in the stratification at each end of the comparison and for each object is accurately observed and recorded. Very few of the objects found in the early campaigns of excavation of Troy can meet this test.

So far as the Early Bronze Age is concerned, no Trojan objects have been reported as found in Egypt, and no Egyptian objects are known from Troy. In Central Anatolia and in Cilicia some characteristically Trojan pots or imitations of them have been recovered; but they may be taken to show only a general synchronism, for the types represented have a long period of use at Troy, extending through ten or 12, or even more phases – probably three or four centuries – and more precise dating is precluded.

With the Cyclades the Trojans apparently had more intimate contacts: distinctive objects from the islands – obsidian, marble idols and vessels, bone tubes and other artifacts, and pottery – make their appearance relatively freely at Troy, and a few Trojan pots of equally distinctive shapes are known from Syros as well as from the Greek mainland. These relations with the Aegean continued to be maintained in the Middle Bronze Age, probably more intensively than before, but there seems to have been a falling off in intercourse with the East. In any event, so far as is known to me, not one single Hittite import has been recognised from any stratified deposit at Troy, and conversely, characteristic Trojan objects have not been found in deposits at the principal Hittite centres.

The same state of affairs evidently prevailed in the Late Bronze Age: little or no direct contact with Central Anatolia, but considerable contacts with the Aegean. Imported Mycenaean pottery recovered at Troy represents the full, inclusive sequence from Late Helladic I to Late Helladic III, and wares of Mycenaean III A and III B were clearly brought from continental Greece in considerable quantities.

From the archaeological point of view, then, it is safe to say that the broad synchronisms with the Early, Middle, and Late epochs of the Aegean Bronze Age have been firmly established. With reference to more detailed dating in actual years – for the most part largely conjectural – further comments will appear in the pertinent chapters that follow.

CHAPTER III

The Early Bronze Age: Troy I

To the early bronze age must be assigned Troy I, II, III, IV, and V. The stratified deposit representing these five periods had a total thickness of some 12 m., and in it could be differentiated as many as 30 strata, almost all marked by architectural remains – that is, by the foundations, walls, and floors of dwelling-houses, each one of which was built, occupied for a time, and ultimately in some manner destroyed before its successor was in turn superposed over the ruins. We have no reliable means of determining with any exactness the duration in years of these many successive phases of habitation; but the imposing mass of debris that accumulated gradually with its numerous subdivisions surely points to a long chronology. In not a few instances multiple floor-levels indicated that some of those houses had often been renovated. An estimate of at least one generation would seem to be a minimum average for each phase – and this is a guess probably far on the short side. It is likely that the Early Bronze Age at Troy lasted not less than a millennium, possibly much longer.

Figs. 4, 5, 6

Through this whole era, whatever its length, a process of constant, slow change and development made itself felt in the steadily evolving civilisation of the town, and there is no sign of a cultural break. It looks as if the people who first established their dominion over the site were able to maintain themselves through many centuries without being conquered and subjected by invaders from outside and forced to alter their customs and way of life. There were undoubtedly many minor accidents and upsets as well as major disasters, but each time the community managed to preserve its life, recover its strength, and resume its progress. The major catastrophes are reflected in the general destruction of all the houses in the settlement as a result of fire, earthquake, storm, or other calamity; and these are recognisable in the widespread wreckage that marked the divisions between Troy I and II, II and III, III and IV, and IV and V. The less serious afflictions, perhaps often local in scope and not extending over the whole site, are represented by the successive strata within each of the principal layers. But even in these less serious disturbances many houses were sometimes completely demolished and had to be replaced.

TROY I

The earliest inhabitants to install themselves on the site built their houses on or just above native rock at the western end of the ridge. It has not yet been determined whence these settlers came. Excavations at Kum Tepe, a low mound that rises on the left bank of the Scamander, not far from the small estuary through which the stream empties into the Dardanelles, have revealed remains of the same culture as that represented in Troy I; but at Kum Tepe the deposit is much deeper and the lower strata may clearly be assigned to a stage earlier than any yet known at Troy itself. Kum Tepe might well be the place where an enterprising band of migrants, arriving by ship, made good their first foothold on the land. No evidence has yet been brought to light to indicate that they encountered any human predecessors in occupation of the plain. Finding the new home to their liking and apparently without the need of forcible conquest, they could have consolidated their position in peace and at leisure. In the course of time, perhaps learning from experience that the spot was low-lying and subject to frequent destructive inundations, they may have judged it advisable to move their main installation to the much more favourably situated higher ground of the ridge on the eastern side of the river valley. A local shift of this kind is plausible enough, but it gives no answer to the question of the remoter origin of the immigrants.

A suggestion made long ago is still tenable: that the arrival of these settlers formed one wave of a large-scale movement of peoples, coming by sea from the southeast and slowly rolling northward along the west coast of Asia Minor as well as westward across the Aegean, where intermediate islands provided stepping-stones to Crete and the Greek mainland. Some archaeologists, at any rate, believe that an underlying kinship is recognisable between the Early Bronze Age cultures of the western Anatolian littoral and those of the Aegean.

The deepest levels at Kum Tepe have yielded no trace of metals. The typical pottery from the oldest deposits shows some features – especially in the profiles of rims – that are characteristic elsewhere of the Late Stone Age. It may therefore be concluded that the new settlers at the time of their coming were still living in a neolithic stage of culture. Subsequently, when they moved inland to the site on the more elevated ridge, they had clearly become acquainted with the knowledge of working copper; and the history of Troy consequently begins with, or early in, the Era of Metals, a stage known in some countries as the Copper Age, but usually called by Aegean archaeologists the beginning of the Early Bronze Age.

The layer of debris that accumulated in Troy I, more than 4 m. thick, was composed of ten strata corresponding to an equal number of successive chronological phases. Nine of the ten excavated in the key area of investigation proved each to contain remains of ruined walls and floors of houses; perhaps it was only by chance that similar architectural remains were not preserved in Stratum Ii.

It was not possible in all parts of the site that were examined to identify and correlate individually these many minor strata, but it proved to be relatively simple everywhere to recognise three successive groups, obviously corresponding to an early, an intermediate, and a late stage of the settlement. In the key area Strata Ia, Ib, and Ic could be assigned to Early I; Id, Ie,

Fig. 7

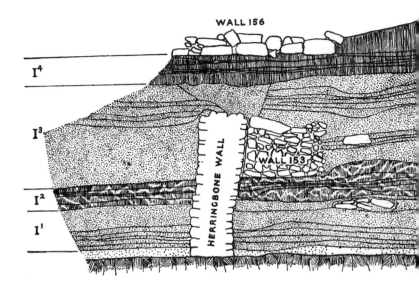

Fig. 7 Diagrammatic section of deposit of Troy I in west bank of Schliemann's North-South Trench

and If to Middle I; Ig, Ih, Ii, and Ij to Late I. These broader divisions within the period – early, middle, and late – are adequate for our purposes. Throughout its history the First Settlement shows a continuity of culture and an unbroken gradual development. A study of the objects recovered reveals extremely little change from any one stratum to the next. Even from the Early Subperiod to the Middle, and from the Middle to the Late, the differences are not startlingly great. If the remains of Early I are compared with those of Late I, however, it becomes obvious that culture did not stand still, but was affected by slow growth and evolution.

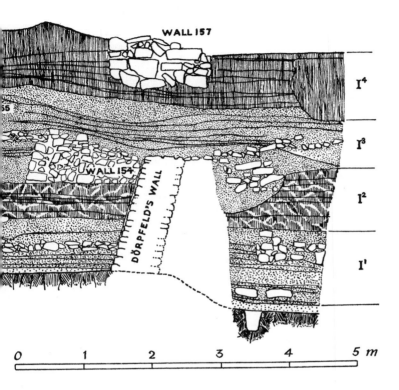

WALL 157

WALL 154

DÖRPFELD'S WALL

I⁴

I³

I²

I'

0   1   2   3   4   5 *m*

The construction of a fortification wall in the very first phase of occupation set its stamp on the settlement and marks it out from all other known contemporary sites in the region as the capital of the northwestern corner of Asia Minor. This dominating character was maintained through many subsequent periods and centuries. Though scanty, the existing remains of the wall that was built in the initial phase of Troy I are unmistakable. Founded on native rock, they were first uncovered by Schliemann in his great North-South Trench, and, despite their dilapidated condition, were correctly interpreted by Dörpfeld, who records the thickness of the wall as about 2.50 m.

Fig. 7

and the length of the relatively short segment as some 12 m. Its distinctive feature is the considerable batter of its outer face (here turned toward the south), a characteristic that presents itself in all the succeeding fortification walls down to the end of Troy VIIa. It has not been possible to explore adequately the farther extent of this earliest defensive wall, but there can be no real doubt that it once encircled the entire citadel.

The early settlement prospered and grew in population and strength; to meet the need for expansion in the Middle Sub-period of Troy I the enclosure was considerably enlarged. A new and more imposing fortification wall was built some 6 m. or more outside the line of its predecessor. It has been followed and partly exposed to view, or traced by means of small pits and tunnels, along the southern and eastern sides of the citadel, through an extent of about 115 m., and has almost everywhere in its course been found still standing to a height of 3.50 m. Its foundations were not carried down to native rock but rested on a thick deposit of debris that had accumulated in the Early Subperiod. Solidly built of rubble, with many large stones used in the lower courses and smaller ones in the upper, the wall seems to have been more than 3 m. thick near the top. The outer face has a strong batter varying from 0.30 to 0.40 m. in a height of 1 m. The rough stonework offered many toe-holds to make climbing easy for aggressive assailants; but there is evidence to show that the sloping podium was crowned by a vertical parapet made of crude brick which was surely too high to be easily scaled. In the middle of the southern side is an imposing gateway: the entrance, 1.97 m. wide, was flanked to right and left by a massive projecting angular tower, the broad top of each giving the defenders an advantageous position for repelling hostile attacks on the gateway below. Remains of a corresponding tower on the eastern side of the acropolis suggest that there may have been another gateway in that direction, and it is not impossible that a third portal opened

Fig. 8

Plate 8

Plate 9

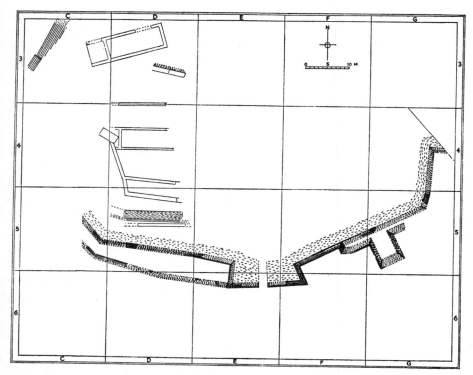

Fig. 8 Fortification of Early, Middle and Late I, house and house walls of Early I

toward the west. It looks as if the stronghold was laid out in accordance with a well-thought-out plan.

In the Late Subperiod of Troy I there was a further expansion of the citadel, and a new fortification wall was erected some 2.50 to 5 m. outside the one it replaced. It exhibits a notable change in the technique of construction: a huge embankment of earth and clay was heaped up nearly 4 m. high, its outer face having a batter with a slope of about 45 degrees. This inclined surface was faced with a single veneer-like layer

Plate 10

of rough stones which were held in place by, and coated with, an application of clay. A rampart of this kind could of course be climbed without difficulty; and, though the evidence is for the most part lacking, it must be assumed that a superposed breastwork of crude brick rose vertically to halt the advance of an attacking enemy. Several segments of this new wall, un‑covered in trial excavations at intervals, show that it extended around the southern, western, and northern, and probably also the eastern border of the fortress.

In all phases of Early, Middle, and Late I the interior of the citadel was occupied by dwelling‑houses of various shapes and sizes. Since it has been possible to examine thoroughly only small areas here and there in this deep‑lying layer, nothing much can be said about the plan of the settlement as a whole. It may be noted, however, that from beginning to end there is no evidence pointing to undue crowding: separate free‑standing houses seem to be the rule. Schliemann found many parallel

Plate 7

walls in his great North‑South Trench, and the houses may have been arranged in a regular system of alignment, but whether they were accessible from properly laid‑out streets or not remains undetermined; no roads leading in from the gate‑ways have been traced.

The central part of the site, where the residence of the ruler presumably stood, could not be excavated, since it was covered by the chief buildings of Troy II, which had to be preserved. The remains of the other houses, farther to the north and west, are scanty and it is hazardous to venture broad generalisations about house plans. With few exceptions, however, each of the houses yet known seems to have consisted of a single room, which had but one doorway, usually in a narrow end. In one or two instances there was a portico through which one passed to reach the door. We have no evidence for windows. The roof was probably flat, made of clay and thatch. One wall of Early I is well known for its herringbone style of masonry; the latter can have had no decorative purpose, for when finished the wall was coated with thick mud plaster.

One of the earliest houses, belonging to Troy Ia, had an apsidal addition at one end; it may have been a small open court. The best preserved house, uncovered in the stratum of Troy Ib, is relatively large, 18.75 m. long and 7 m. wide. It was oriented from northeast to southwest with its front entrance facing the setting sun. A deep portico gave access to a door⁄way, not accurately centred, which opened into a long narrow room, with a hard clay floor. The latter had been many times renewed, gradually raising the level by some 0.50 m. In the centre of the room was an open hearth of irregular shape, roughly paved with small flat stones, which had been partly calcined by the heat of many fires. A second and smaller hearth came to light in the southeastern quarter, and not far from it was a shallow clay⁄lined pit that had possibly served as a receptacle for the setting of bread dough, an arrangement familiar still today in some houses in Turkish villages. An abundance of animal bones and sea shells in this end of the room indicated that it was a place for cooking and eating. A low stone platform, large enough for a divan, was fitted against the wall in the northeastern corner of the chamber; and a broader, longer construction of the same kind, adequate for a double bed, stood close to the wall near the northwest corner. The house contained no other fixed furniture. Traces of plaited matting were observed on the floor. Chairs and tables had presumably not yet been invented, and the occupants of the house no doubt sat on rugs or skins laid on the floor.

Scattered about in the room were some bits of badly corroded copper, two primitive idols of marble, two polishers, a whet⁄stone, and six saddle querns; ten awls or pins made of bone, two fangs of a dog, pierced for stringing – perhaps as amulets – four whorls or buttons of terracotta; and a good deal of broken pottery from which it was possible to reconstruct six pots.

Plate 12

Fig. 8

Plate 13

Plate 14

A custom that prevailed in the early settlements at Troy is illustrated by two infant-burials found just beneath the floor of the house, one an inhumation in a shallow pit covered by a flat stone, the other an interment in a broken pottery-urn. Four graves of the same kind were exposed in the open space immediately to the north of the house. There were no objects accompanying these burials. In all instances the bones were those of new-born babes, and the skeletons were in too disintegrated a state to give much useful anthropological information. They do, however, offer testimony that the rate of infant mortality was relatively high in early Troy.

In its design the house just described exhibits some distinctive features: free-standing position, porch and doorway at one short end, and a single large rectangular chamber, with a central hearth. Some of its contemporary neighbours as well as some antecedents in Troy Ia were probably of the same type, and they may fairly be regarded as forerunners of the much larger structures of the Second Settlement, called by Dörpfeld *Megara* II A, II B, and II R. It has sometimes been thought that the *megaron* was introduced into the Aegean area by invaders coming from the north. Whatever its original home, this distinctive type of building, as demonstrated by the new evidence at Troy, is now seen to have been firmly established in northwestern Asia Minor at the very beginning of the Early Bronze Age, and the theory of its European origin is no longer easily maintainable.

It is not necessary here to describe in detail the remains of houses and habitation-deposits of the same general kinds that were found in all the successive superposed strata which were called Ic, Id, and so on to Ij. Each revealed itself as continuing directly the culture of its predecessor; there were almost imperceptible changes from one phase to the next, but no sign of any real break in the continuity through Middle and Late I. The final phase, Ij, evidently came to its end in a great fire that destroyed the entire town. An overlying stratum, Ik, consisting of burned debris from that catastrophe, seems to have been spread out over a wide area, probably in a large operation of levelling the ground for the construction of the new citadel which marks the beginning of Troy II.

The inhabitants of Troy I lived a simple but settled life in relatively comfortable, well-built houses. In many, the walls were coated with plaster; and woven mats were laid on the floors. As already mentioned, there was little or no furniture in the modern sense. Fixed hearths presumably provided for heating in cold weather as well as for cooking. There may have been openings in the roof or high in the walls to allow the smoke to escape. Spit-rests to help in grilling and three-legged pots that could stand over the fire were included in the kitchen equipment. From the debris of food left on the floor we see that the ordinary diet was not without variety. Beef, mutton or lamb, goat and pork seem to have been in staple supply, varied occasionally with rabbit and venison. Dolphin, tunny, and other fish, along with unidentified wild fowl were likewise eaten, as well as many kinds of mussels from the sea. By the Late Subperiod of Troy I – if not indeed much earlier – wheat was evidently already well on the way to becoming the staff of life.

Knives and forks for use at the dining table (as well as the table itself) had not yet been thought of, but fingers could be supplemented by simple cutting implements of copper, stone, and bone. Stone vessels and pottery made of clay in a wide variety of shapes – for many different purposes – were in constant use, contributing to the amenities of living.

What kind of clothing was worn is a matter of deduction and speculation. Skins and leather were available and were doubtless used. But the spindle whorls and loom weights that have Plate 15, *Fig. 9* been found imply that spinning and weaving were familiar occupations in the earliest Trojan households. Sheep and goats

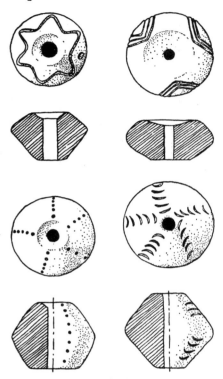

Fig. 9 Decorated whorls of Troy I

must have supplied wool for yarn, and homespun fabrics may surely be postulated. Some of the whorls of terracotta were probably made to serve as buttons, and garments could also have been fastened with copper or bone pins many of which have been recovered. Two slender copper needles with eye-holes for yarn or thin cord give ground for believing that the women of Troy I were equipped for more than the coarsest kind of sewing.

No objects of gold or silver have yet been discovered in strata of Troy I, but the failure to find them may be fortuitous and does not necessarily mean that such things did not exist. Articles of personal adornment that have been brought to light comprise simple modest elements, such as spherical beads of jade-like or other kinds of stone, small amulets of marble or other limestone of various shapes but usually pierced for suspension or stringing; a necklace made of seven bird-bones perforated near one end for threading on a cord, but otherwise unworked; and two canine teeth with neatly drilled string-holes. All these may have been ornaments worn by women.

Fig. 10

The men of Troy I naturally possessed weapons of stone and probably of metal. No actual example in copper has come from a certified stratigraphic context but a deposit of the Middle Subperiod yielded a fragment of a terracotta mould for casting a dagger blade or spearhead which was made rigid by a strong rounded midrib. This is obviously a developed type that implies considerable prior experimenting. That metal knives were also in use may be deduced from the recovery of several whetstones.

Ribs of cattle were sometimes worked into the form of blades with sharp edges. Although in some instances they resemble figurines, they would certainly serve well as cutting implements. Bits of flint with serrated edges and acutely sharpened points may be from arrows or small javelins; one example has two tiny sockets drilled transversely, undoubtedly for rivets or pins to fasten a shaft. Small rounded pellets of stone could have served as missiles thrown with a sling. Several hammer-axes, complete or broken, and a double hammer, each provided with a well-drilled hole for a handle, may likewise be counted among the weapons of the period.

Broad round celts and narrow, flat, chisel-like celts should perhaps be reckoned as tools, and to this category may be assigned numerous blades and flakes of flint, several polishing stones, as well as a great many awls or pins and various other implements of bone. Worthy of special mention is a well-preserved sturdy hook of copper from the deepest stratum. Though rectangular in section, not very sharp, and made without a barb, it was almost surely used as a fishhook.

Plate 15

Plate 15

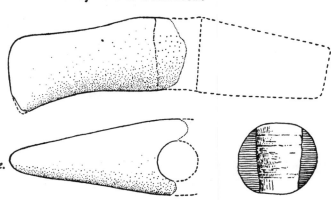

Fig. 10 Hammer-axe of stone. Middle Phase of Troy I

Among the surviving remains of Troy I – as at virtually all other early sites – pottery occurs in the greatest preponderance; and these products, both in fabric and form, bear a distinctive character of their own. All pots were shaped by hand without the use of the potter's wheel. As a whole this ware, from beginning to end of Troy I, may fairly be called a dark monochrome fabric. The colour ranges from almost jet black to grey and olive green, relieved occasionally by pieces in brown, tan, and – more rarely – even red. An olive-green tint is especially characteristic in the Early Subperiod; darker hues are more common in Middle I; and a true black enjoys greater vogue in Late I, when a distinctive smooth lustre-ware, usually jet-black, but sometimes wine-red, makes its appearance. Through all three subperiods there are many gradations in quality from fine to coarse. Upwards of 60 more or less different

Fig. 11 *Characteristic pottery shapes of Troy I*

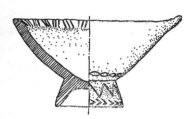 

Fig. 12 Pots with incised decoration, Troy

shapes of vessels have been recognised, many clearly designed to be used in eating and drinking, some for pouring liquids, others for storage, and yet others for cooking and more special purposes. A good many additional shapes are undoubtedly represented among the masses of fragments insufficiently pre‑served for us to assemble and mend.

Fig. 11

In the Early Subperiod shallow bowls differentiated by a peculiar thickening of the inside of the rim are fairly common, along with shallow, sharply angular bowls, similar vessels supported on a high, spreading hollow foot, jugs with slanting beaks or with high spouts and with the back of the neck cut away toward the handle. In Middle I, bowls with thickened rim give way to a modified form with less pronounced thicken‑ing, while, alongside the still prolific angular bowls, a new type with curving profile begins to be popular. In Late I, pedestal‑bowls virtually disappear, and the bowls with curving sides become predominant. Throughout the many successive phases of the settlement the pottery thus exhibits slow gradual change in an uninterrupted development.

Fig. 12

From the outset to the end of Troy I it was mainly a sombre undecorated ware; but in all subperiods – especially in the earliest – it was occasionally brightened by decorative patterns executed in a variety of techniques. One plastic type had lumps

Figs. 12, 13
Plate 16, *Fig. 14*

Fig. 13 Incised patterns on rims of bowls, Troy I

or strips of clay applied, often forming rectilinear or curvilinear patterns, sometimes suggesting features of human faces. Ribbed, grooved, fluted, and punched designs also occur. Incision is, however, the predominantly employed technique, seen most often on the inside of rims in numerous straight or curving linear, geometrical motifs, including the swastika, which were usually made to stand out conspicuously by a filling of white matter. Human features are occasionally represented. Much more rarely this light-on-dark decoration was achieved in a different way by the direct application of white paint (now dull and rather fugitive) to the surface of the pot. Simple patterns of parallel lines, vertical, horizontal, or diagonal, are usual.

That considerable progress toward major art had already been made in Troy I is shown by the discovery – in a stratum at least as early as the Middle Subperiod – of what may fairly be called a monumental sculptured stele. Made of grey, flaky, friable limestone, it had been re-used as material in the building of a barrier in Middle I. The stone, which once had a tapering form, had been much damaged, the lower part broken away, and the sculptured surface badly worn. It is now 0.62 m. wide at the top and is preserved to a height of 0.79 m. The original height is unknown. Near the top of the stele a heart-shaped face, represented in frontal view, was carved in low relief. The face is countersunk within a fairly broad, flat, raised outline; this latter, rising from an almost pointed chin, frames on each side rounded cheeks, then turns sharply inward to form arching eyebrows that meet and join, to continue downward as a thick flat nose. The hair seems to have been parted in the middle, and a lock falls down on each side to right and left. A row of shallow drilled holes in each lock may have been intended for fastening decorative attachments of some kind, or – since they are hardly deep enough to hold anything – they may merely emphasise the texture of the hair. The right eye is indicated by curved lines above and below; the left was presumably shown in the same way, but damage has obliterated all evidence. A

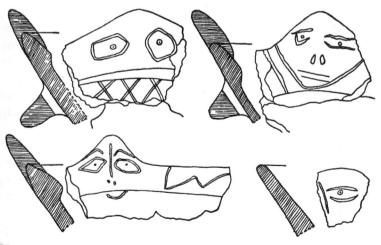

ig. 14 Representations of faces on rim projections of bowls, Troy I

short V-shaped slot below the nose renders a narrow mouth.
To the left of the face (as one views it) is carved in broad
flattish relief what may be the staff of a mace or a club, perhaps
with a spherical head. Traces of carving below and to the right
of the face are too badly damaged to be interpreted.

The stele was obviously designed to be set upright, with the
relief exposed to view. Whether it was a secular memorial
erected by some ruler or noble, or a tombstone placed over a
grave, or a monument connected with a cult must remain an
open question. The heraldic nature of the design might be
taken to suggest the first of these possibilities. The third is
favoured by the fact that two other stone slabs, which had been
re-used in the same barrier with the stele, seem to be tables of
offerings that probably once had their place in a shrine. The
use of the stone to mark the tomb of some distinguished person
cannot be ruled out, but parallels for such a purpose at so early
a stage in the Aegean area are not yet known.

Whatever its character, the relief is the oldest sculptured
monument yet found in Western Anatolia. It does not look
like a first primitive attempt to carve stone. The rather formal,
conventionalised or stylised design implies a long preceding
period of experiment and development. Representations of
human features in the same general style occur already on the
pottery recovered in strata belonging to the Early Subperiod of
Troy I, and they continue to appear in Late I and in the
familiar face-pots of Troy II and later. The stele consequently
holds its place in the evolution of Trojan art. Its startling
resemblance to certain stone carvings that have been discovered
in contexts of the Stone Age in southern France and the region
of the Marne has not yet been satisfactorily explained. Any
direct connection between those far-distant areas and Troy in the
Neolithic Period or in the Early Bronze Age is surely unlikely.

So far as concerns the religious side of life in Troy I, the
evidence available is scanty, difficult to recognise, and not easy

Fig. 14

o interpret. The two crude tables of offerings, which have
•een mentioned above, were probably appurtenances of a
hrine, and their appearance at Troy recalls analogous cult-
urniture at Sesklo, and in Minoan Crete. The deposits of
Troy I have produced fairly numerous figurines or idols made
f marble or other stone, several of bone, and at least one of
:rracotta. By and large, although by no means exactly identical,
ey bear an undeniable general resemblance to the figurines of
e 'amorphous' type familiar from Cycladic sites of the Early
Aegean Bronze Age. In both regions they seem to have been
res and penates, cherished in each household. The widely
iffused occurrence in private houses in primitive civilisations
f idols of various types, but predominantly female, has fre-
uently been taken to indicate the prevalence of fertility cults;
nd this explanation is not unlikely at Troy.

No adult burials of Troy I have ever been found, and little
an be said about burial customs. Schliemann reports the dis-
overy in a stratum resting on native rock of two urns which
ontained the bones of infants; and two similar urn-burials,
ogether with four infant inhumations of Phase Ib were brought
o light by the Cincinnati Expedition. From Early or Middle
there is also a grave that contained the skeleton of a child of
ome 11 years. Schliemann believed he could recognise in the
rns, in addition to the infant's bones, ashes from the burned
ones of the mothers of the children; but this observation has
ot been confirmed by later excavations. Burials, either simple
nhumations or in large jars, are known from other sites in
vestern Asia Minor, more or less nearly contemporary with
Troy I, such as Babaköy, Yortan, Bozüyük, Soma, and, farther
nland, Kusura. It is not improbable that Trojan custom was
imilar, but the burial-places have so far eluded discovery.

Troy is the only habitation-site in northwestern Asia Minor
hat has yet been excavated on an adequate scale. As indicated
•y sporadic finds and graves, further explorations will prob-

Plate 15

Plate 18

ably show that the culture we call Trojan was widely spread over a relatively broad area in this part of Anatolia, extending certainly as far eastward as Erdek, Balikesir, Babaköy, Soma and Yortan, and probably much farther southward in the western coastal zone and its hinterland. The culture of Troy is represented across the Dardanelles in a habitation site where the 'tumulus of Protesilaos' stands. The same civilisation has also been revealed at Thermi on Lesbos, where its evolution through five successive phases, or towns, was followed in the admirable excavations of Miss W. Lamb. A closely related, if not identical, culture with an early stage going back into Neolithic times, and with houses and a magnificent fortification wall, has been uncovered by the Italian School of Archaeology at Poliochni on the island of Lemnos.

This widespread culture was apparently independent and self-sustaining, resembling in some ways but different from the contemporary culture in Central Anatolia. Its external relations seem to have been mainly with the west, that is, with the Cyclades and the mainland of Greece, as well as with Thrace and Macedonia. Perhaps there were ties of kinship with the people across the Aegean.

Chapter IV

The Early Bronze Age: Troy II

TROY II BEGAN with a complete reconstruction of the citadel after the disaster that had brought the First Settlement to its end. There is no evidence of a break or of any appreciable chronological gap; on the contrary the culture of Troy I seems to pass with uninterrupted continuity into that of Troy II. The destruction by fire that reduced the houses of Phase Ij to ruins was apparently only an internal calamity, more intensified than those which had so often occurred before and which in their stratified debris provide the physical evidence for the successive stages of Troy I.

The Second Settlement was excavated in almost its entire extent by Schliemann; it was later re-examined and interpreted by Dörpfeld whose conclusions were based mainly on a searching observation and study of the surviving stratified architectural remains. Dörpfeld was able to differentiate three principal phases, each marked by the construction of a new fortification wall; and within this stronghold he recognised the ruined walls of three corresponding sets of buildings, superposed one above the other. To the third of these phases he assigned the palatial *megaron*, familiar on all plans of Troy, together with several other large houses of the same general type. The more recent researches of the Cincinnati Expedition revealed that the Second Settlement maintained its existence through four further phases, during which the *megaron* apparently continued to be occupied, before the entire citadel was again laid waste in another tremendous fire. It was this terminal burned stratum that Schliemann long believed to represent Homeric Troy. He had first attributed it to the Third City; but later, when Dörpfeld became his associate, he reassigned it to the third phase of the Second City. With the results of the most recent excava-

Fig. 15

tions it is now possible to differentiate seven strata which may be designated IIa, IIb, IIc and so on to IIg. These seven strata, though in some places much compressed, make up a layer that varies in thickness from 2 to 3 m. and more. Foundations of buildings and house walls were fairly well preserved in several of the seven strata, and all contained at least some architectural elements. The sequence is therefore clearly established.

Roughly circular in plan and about 110 m. in diameter, the new citadel was only a little larger than its predecessor, but the powerful defensive wall and the remains of substantial houses inside the enclosure make it clear that Troy II continued to maintain its character as the stronghold of a ruler dominating the northwestern Troad.

The fortification wall erected at the beginning of Phase IIa, though of modest proportions, was more massive than its forerunner of Troy Ij. It has been traced only along the southern half of the circuit; on the northern side it was apparently in large part incorporated in the wall of Phase IIc. In the section still preserved on the south the lower part of the wall, which was built of relatively small unworked stones and had a broadly sloping outer face, rose to a height of some 3 m.; its flat top, about 2.70 m. wide, supported a vertical superstructure of crude brick, no doubt once equally high, and coated with mud plaster. Small, rectangular projecting towers at intervals of approximately 10 m. strengthened the defensive arrangements. In some places the wall is seen to have been built not as a single homogeneous structure but in two separate parallel components, an inner and an outer unit, divided by a joint and not held together by bonding. Whether this is to be explained as a technical peculiarity of construction or as evidence of two building-periods is not altogether certain. But the remains of houses inside the citadel show that what we call Phase IIa must actually represent two chronological stages.

Two principal gateways were recognised by Dörpfeld, one

n the west, the other on the south; there may have been a third
nd a fourth on the east and the north. The two that have
urvived display a peculiar plan; each has the form of a fairly
ong covered corridor, or passage, which ran directly underneath a huge tower, jutting out from the wall, and each gradu-
lly ascended toward the ground level inside the citadel. The
ides of the passage were shored with vertical timbers set fairly
lose together; they presumably also supported transverse beams
o prevent the stonework of the tower from falling into the
orridor.

In the reconstruction that inaugurated Phase IIb the fortifi-
ation wall along the southern flank of the citadel was shifted
utward some 6 or 7 m., thereby increasing the area enclosed.
The wall itself, in its stone substructure and crude brick super-
tructure, was similar to its precursor. But the lower part was
uilt in a more orderly style of masonry, the stones of its
xterior facing being laid in neat, almost uniform courses. The
lan of the enceinte as a whole also seems to have acquired
nore regularity, apparently designed as a more or less nearly
ymmetrical polygon with straight sides, roughly 26 m. long,
ach angle marked by a projecting tower. The course of the
vall along the northerly brow of the hill has not been certainly
dentified; it, too, was presumably merged into the succeeding
tructure of Phase IIc. The two earlier gateways on the south
nd west were adjusted to the new wall and continued to be
sed, the western one being provided with a small lateral sally-
ort. A postern gate of no great size appears in the huge tower
nat formed the extreme western angle of the fortress.

The project of general rebuilding which ushered in the third
hase of Troy II was carried out on a grand scale, and the
ortification wall now took on an imposing aspect. Along the
outhern side of the citadel, and probably along the eastern as
vell, it was again moved outward some 5 to 10 m. beyond the
rlier line, and the space within was thus enlarged.

Plate **19**

The new wall does not show a uniform homogeneous style
of masonry. Along the eastern flank it was founded on earth
and had a vertical stone socle about 1 m. high. On this rested
a superstructure of crude brick some 4 m. thick, which was
found still standing to a height of 3 m. Rectangular towers
about 3.80 m. wide and projecting 2.25 m., added to the
defensive strength. Farther northward the new wall was evidently founded on the earlier works of Troy IIb and IIa.
Along the northern edge of the hill, however, there is now a
broad gap, more than 70 m. wide, in which no trace of the
wall remains. This marks the place where Schliemann in his
earliest campaigns opened up his wide 'platform'. At each
extremity of this terrace the truncated end of the great wall of
Phase IIc appears, supported on the ruins of its predecessors.
Beyond the gap the continuation of the wall has been traced
and exposed around the western and southern periphery. The
western sector shows a carelessly built stone socle surmounted
by brickwork, and there are no towers. In this section Dörpfeld
recognised two periods of construction: in the first the wall was
relatively thin and was strengthened by buttresses on the inner
side; in the second the thickness was increased to 4 m., and
buttresses were no longer required. Both periods were assigned
by Dörpfeld to Phase IIc.

The great western tower of Phase IIb had fallen into ruin
and had been covered by debris; it was replaced by a plain
angle, rising to a much higher level. Just beyond the turn was
a small sally-port. Along the southern perimeter the stone socle
of the wall is well preserved, founded wherever possible on the
underlying earlier structure. It is relatively low and has only
moderate batter on its exterior face. The two earlier principal
gateways of Phases IIa and IIb, now dismantled and filled in
with earth and rubbish, were replaced by two larger and more
stately entrances, each shifted some 10 m. eastward from the
position of its predecessor.

The southwestern gateway was approached from outside by
a monumental ascending ramp more than 21 m. long, 7.55 m.
wide, and bordered on each side by a stone wall, probably
breast-high. The roadway, which was paved with great slabs
of limestone, rose some 5 m. to the level of the gateway at a
gradient of approximately one in four, too steep for wheeled
traffic. The actual portal at the top of the ramp was a tripartite
building, comprising a central room between an inner and an
outer portico. The lateral walls of the inner porch terminated in
antae which were fitted with shaped stone bases for wooden
parastades. This is a distinctive architectural feature of Phase
Ic, as Dörpfeld observed.

The southeastern gateway, though of greater dimensions,
exhibits essentially the same plan as the southwestern, except
that no ramp was needed, since the ground in this place falls
off in a gentle slope toward the plateau. Here again we have an
outer and an inner porch, separated by a central hall, which
was provided with a closable door at each end. Both gateways
give evidence of minor repairs and remodellings apparently
carried out on several occasions; they probably represent altera-
tions effected in the later phases of Troy II.

Those who passed through the southeastern gateway entered
a cobble-paved outer court more than 12 m. wide, from which
they could no doubt turn to right or left along the inner side
of the fortification wall. Continuing straight ahead, however,
they reached, in the northerly boundary wall of the court, a
small gateway about 8 m. long and 5 m. wide. This little
building, resembling a classical Greek propylon, comprised
an outer and an inner portico separated by a cross wall in which
was a central doorway. A great stone threshold block, still
in situ, bears evidence that the door-opening was 1.82 m. wide;
the door itself was probably made of wood with two leaves,
swinging to right and left. The outer portico is nearly twice as
deep as the inner; neither seems to have had a central column.

The side walls at each extremity end in a worked stone base which clearly supported a wooden casing, forming the anta The whole little gateway was probably covered by a flat clay or earthen roof, supported on transverse tree-trunks or wooden beams.

The inner, pebble-covered court into which the propylon led was bordered on the southwest and southeast – perhaps also on the northeast – by a stone wall about 1 m. thick. To the eastward of the propylon the wall is strengthened at fairly regular intervals of some 3.25 m. by sturdy buttresses, which project nearly 1.30 m. into the inner court, and about half as much into the outer one. On the western side of the gateway similar buttresses are spaced somewhat more widely, and wooden columns were apparently set up between each pair

Plate 20

One properly shaped stone base for such a column was found still in its original position at the southern angle of the court It is therefore clear that a colonnade, which must have been roofed, ran around the sides of this inner court – another anticipation of an architectural design that reached its highest development in much later times.

Opposite the propylon, across the court, but not exactly centred along the same axis, stood the most imposing building of all those within the citadel. This is the great *megaron*, which Dörpfeld designated II A on his plan. Its northern end and the greater part of its western side were destroyed in the digging of Schliemann's North-South Trench, and many details of plan and construction are irretrievably lost. The total length of the edifice and the form of its northern façade can only be conjectured. The walls had a foundation of large unworked stones carried up high enough to form an adequate socle on which was built a massive superstructure of crude brick, about 1.45 m. thick. These walls, which were reinforced by a framework of horizontal, and perhaps also vertical, timbers, with numerous transverse struts, ended toward the south in well

Fig. 15

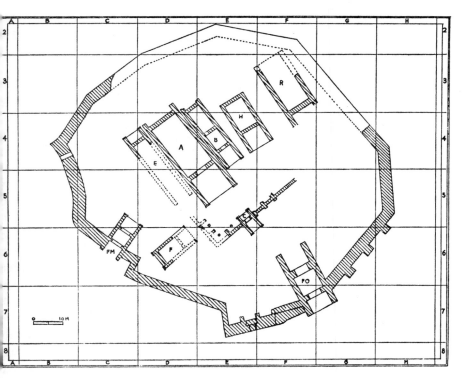

ig. 15 Plan of citadel in Phase IIc

nade antae. They were faced with wooden parastades, formed
f six upright timbers that stood on specially shaped stone
ases. Both inside and out, the walls were presumably coated
vith clay plaster.

The *megaron* took the form of a spacious portico, facing the
ourt to the southeast, and behind it evidently a great hall of
tate. The porch, 10.20 m. wide, and almost equally deep from
ront to back, was approximately square in plan. No column
ase came to light in the façade, but the span is so great that

65

one or two substantial posts or pillars to support the roof may surely be postulated. Shaped stone bases, like the one found in the court, which apparently rested on earth without a proper foundation, may easily have been removed in a later period by seekers of building material.

The doorway, about 4 m. wide, leading from the portico into the main hall, had no stone threshold, but was probably fitted with wooden jambs on both sides. The opening may have been closed by heavy hangings rather than by swinging double doors, since there were no signs of pivot-sockets.

The hall of state, of the same width as the portico, was at least 16 m. long, perhaps even 20 m. or more. It had a floor of hard-packed clay. Wooden columns to hold up the ceiling and roof were almost essential in so large a room; though no actual evidence of such supports was recognised by Dörpfeld, it may have perished when the building was burned down, or possibly was missed in Schliemann's early excavations. Centred along the main axis of the hall some 7 m. distant from the doorway, Dörpfeld observed remains of a circular platform of clay, rising 0.07 m. above the floor. Enough was preserved to permit the original diameter to be calculated at approximately 4 m. The part that has survived is a segment of the outer edge of a stepped open hearth, an early forerunner of the similar ceremonial hearths now known in the Mycenaean palaces at Mycenae, Tiryns, and Pylos. No traces of other fixed or movable furniture were observed in the room. There must surely have been a special seat or throne for the king, perhaps stools or benches of wood or stone for the members of his family and council. The floor was no doubt covered with matting, carpets or skins.

The superstructure of the *megaron* is gone, and we can only speculate about its exact form. The roof was probably flat, made of a thick, heavy layer of clay and reeds laid on stout horizontal wooden beams placed close together; and if there were no columns in the hall and portico, the transverse timbers must have been of imposing dimensions to bear the enormous weight. A clerestory, directly above the hearth, to admit light and air is conceivable; failing that, there may have been at least an aperture to let the smoke out. A raised gallery, running around the sides of the room, is not beyond the realm of possibility. We are left equally uncertain about the manner in which the building ended toward the northwest and about its length. Behind the great hall there is room for another chamber, perhaps even for two, but no decisive evidence has survived.

In the grandeur of its proportions as well as in its architectural style and technique, the *megaron* takes first place among the buildings in the citadel of Troy II; and there can be no doubt that it was the seat of the principal personality. Whether it was used mainly for public ceremonial occasions, or was also the actual residence of the ruler and his family, has not been determined. In any event the *megaron* was flanked on each side by a structure of almost identical plan, but designed on a much more modest scale. Both looked out toward the southeast on the same colonnaded entrance court that lay in front of the hall of state. Except for insignificant remains at its northern end, the southwestern unit is wholly lost, since it stood directly in the path of Schliemann's North-South Trench. Its twin on the northeastern side is, however, relatively well preserved, with its deep portico, main hall, and a rear chamber. It seems likely that these two lateral buildings provided living and sleeping quarters for the reigning family. Three other *megara* recognised by Dörpfeld, II H and II R to the northeast of the group already mentioned, and II F to the southwest of the court, were probably also at the disposal of the ruler, who seems to have preferred the distinctive *megaron* plan. Other types of buildings with many small rooms are represented: for example, a fairly large one, called by Dörpfeld II D, stood to the north and west of the Southwestern Gateway. It seems to have had at

Fig. 15

least 12 small chambers, for the most part rectangular in shape. They may have served as storerooms, or to accommodate a garrison or a guard of honour just inside the gate.

The fortification walls and gateways were maintained with minor repairs and alterations until the final catastrophe at the end of Phase IIg. All the *megara*, except II R, evidently also continued to stand and to be occupied through the later phases of Troy II. One of the most striking innovations in Phase IId was the enlargement of the colonnaded court in front of *Megaron* II A. The boundary wall, with its transverse buttresses, was shifted outward some 3 m. and rebuilt in the same style as in Phase IIc. Wooden columns were probably again employed to support a roofed colonnade, although no stone column bases were actually found. But in some of the bays along the westerly side of the court carbonised remains of fallen timbers were recognised, and there were likewise many chunks of clay that still retained impressions of the reeds and branches that had been used in the roofing.

The most notable feature encountered in the stratum of Phase IId was the presence in great numbers of smallish pits of irregular size, shape, and depth. They had been cut through the floors and pavements, and they were usually found to contain fragments of large jars, or *pithoi*, and of slate, together with numerous potsherds, shells, and much rubbish. Some of these cavities were almost certainly used as setting-places for large storage jars which were probably covered by slate lids. Schliemann records that he discovered more than 600 such *pithoi* in the stratum which he attributed to the 'Burnt City'; it is likely that a good many of them really belonged to Phase IId.

Very little has survived to shed light on the state of the community in Phase IIe; but in that and the two succeeding phases, IIf and IIg, considerable innovations appear, perhaps reflecting some political, economic, or social changes. The great *megaron* and most of its companions remain, clinging their predominant position; but a complex of house walls ncroaches more and more on the courts that had previously een reserved for the king and his family. These were unpre/ ntious structures of irregular plan, evidently private houses ither than store/chambers connected with the palace. It is kely that similar houses in Phase IIg extended widely through/ ut the citadel, but the evidence was long ago removed.

The stratum of Troy IIg had an average thickness of more lan 1 m.; it consisted mainly of ashes, charred matter, and urned debris. This deposit apparently extended uniformly ver the great *megaron* and across the entire site, eloquent evi/ ence that the settlement perished in a vast conflagration from /hich no buildings escaped ruin. This is the 'Burnt City' of chliemann, who first called it the Third City, later the econd City, and who until 1890 believed it was the Troy of 'riam and Homer.

In all areas examined by the Cincinnati Expedition it was bvious that the catastrophe struck suddenly, without warning, iving the inhabitants little or no time to collect and save their 1ost treasured belongings before they fled. All the houses xposed were still found to contain the fire/scarred wreckage f their furnishings, equipment, and stores of supplies. Almost /ery building yielded scattered bits of gold ornaments and :wellery, no doubt hastily abandoned in panic flight.

Most of the famous 'treasures' recovered by Schliemann may ow safely be attributed to Troy IIg. Nine of the hoards he sts, including the 'Great Treasure', were unearthed in and about dwelling of considerable size (about 8 × 15 m.) which he illed the 'House of the City King'. Comprising five or more ɔoms, it stood just to the north of the southwestern gateway. s style of masonry (walls of crude brick founded on a socle of one) and its place in the stratification permit the conclusion lat the house was built in Phase IIg, and was destroyed in the reat fire that put an end to Troy II.

Plate 22

Whether the disaster was brought about by enemy action or by accident cannot be certainly stated, though there are considerations that point to each of these alternatives. If the city had been captured and razed by conquerors, some of the luckless inhabitants would surely have fallen victims to the attack and an excavator might expect to find in the ruins remains of human skeletons. So far as is ascertainable in the archaeological records, we have actually only one instance in which a fragment of a small adult skull was definitely found in the stratum of Phase IIg. Schliemann mentions the skeletons of 'two warriors' with bronze helmets, found in the burnt layer; but the stratigraphic position is not certified, and the helmets later turned out to be fragments of a bronze vessel. One might therefore conclude that the occupants of the town escaped. On the other hand, if an invading army took the city it would surely have thoroughly looted the houses before putting them to the torch; and few if any 'treasures' of gold and silver would have been left for archaeologists to recover. But again a counter argument might hold that if all or most of the citizens had run away to safety, they would surely have returned sooner or later to recover the treasures they had left behind. Their failure to do so can only be accounted for by assuming that some powerful deterrent prevented their returning. What actually happened to bring about the burning of the whole establishment is still an unsolved mystery, but it is a fact that Troy II was totally destroyed. Another fact is, as we shall see, that the catastrophe caused no recognisable break in the continuity of cultural development on the site: the same civilisation, without perceptible new external influence, marched quietly and steadily on into the succeeding settlement of Troy III.

But first we must attempt to appraise the standard of living that had been achieved in Troy II. It had risen a good deal higher than that of Troy I. More space was available within the citadel and houses were more commodious. Of course the

royal *megara* cannot fairly be used for comparison with what
had preceded them, the corresponding buildings of Troy I being
still unknown. But in the massive style of masonry that now
prevails, with broad stone socle and an almost equally thick
wall of crude brick, there is an impression of strength and
solidity; and a suggestion of greater elegance appears in the fine
finishing coat of white plaster that has survived here and there,
even though no trace of painted decoration has been recognised.
Hearths and braziers continued to serve for heating and cooking,
and spit-rests show that meat was still grilled over the fire as
heretofore. Remains of animal bones and shells indicate that
the same varieties of meat and fish were available as in Troy I,
and that sea food was even more popular and its diversity still
greater. The ruined houses of Phase IIg produced abundant
carbonised remains of beans, lentils or vetch, and wheat, some
of which were found lying in large heaps. Many millstones, for
the most part saddle querns, together with grinders, suggest that
in each household these cereals were crushed and ground as
needed. Life was clearly based on an agricultural economy.

The relatively large flocks of sheep and goats maintained by
the people of Troy II, as attested by the animal bones found in
the debris, may be taken to imply that wool production had
substantially increased. Whorls of terracotta have been recovered in vast numbers, some of them no doubt made for attachment to the ends of spindles. Dörpfeld found an actual spindle
of bone still retaining at one extremity a whorl as it had
originally been fastened. In Treasure M Schliemann recognised carbonised remains of a wooden spindle with thread,
likewise charred, still wound about it. Whether the material
was of wool, linen, or cotton could not be determined.

In addition to spinning, weaving was another regular domestic handicraft. In a house of Phase IIg clear evidence of a
loom was preserved. One end of it was attached to a wall; the
other end, projecting about 1.10 m. into the room, was sup-

Fig. 16

Fig. 17

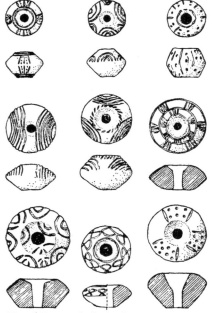

Fig. 16 Decorated whorls of Troy II

ported by two stout wooden posts, 0.25 m. apart, which had
been fixed upright in setting holes that had been cut through the
floor. On the latter, between the post-holes and the wall, lay
three or four rows of clay loom weights just as they had fallen
some had been more or less baked hard by the fire that destroyed
the house. Many had no doubt disintegrated, but one of relatively large size and 14 smaller examples had suffered little or
no damage. It was not possible to ascertain of what material
the textiles woven on this loom were made. The heavy weights
suggest that the warp consisted of thick threads or cords and
that the fabric was coarse, probably of wool. A great many of
the whorls are likely to have served as buttons that could be
slipped through a buttonhole, or loop.

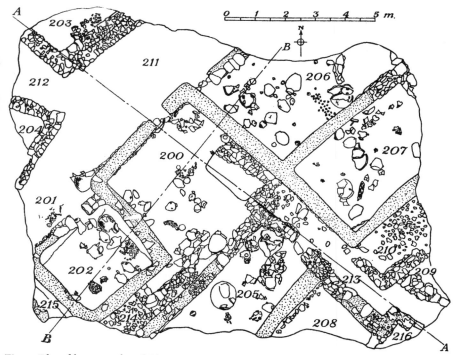

Fig. 17 Plan of house complex of Phase IIg

In the contemporary fire-marked earth and debris about the loom weights 189 small gold beads of 15 different shapes were recovered. Scattered about helter-skelter, they gave no idea of the sequence in which they had originally been strung together, but they probably once formed part of a necklace or bracelet. It is tempting in this confusion and disorder to see reflected the sudden onset of the disastrous fire that swept over the town and laid it in ruins, and the panic-stricken flight that ensued. One can readily imagine a woman engaged in her weaving, having taken off her bracelet and hung it on a peg while she worked, starting up with terror when she heard the fire alarm and running to save her life, leaving her bracelet behind. Or it may have caught in the loom, and the cord may have broken, letting

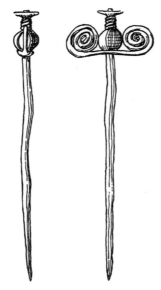

*Fig. 18 Gold pin of
Phase IIg*

the beads fall to be strewn over the floor. There must surely have been many such scenes of minor if not major, drama.

That the material prosperity of the settlement had risen high above the level attained in Troy I is amply demonstrated by the relative abundance of gold and silver in the various strata of Troy II. By far the greater part of these objects of precious metals was found by Schliemann in a series of caches or 'treasures', some 16 of which may almost certainly be attributed to the Second Settlement. His account of the circumstances of discovery is not always adequate to show exactly in which stratum each hoard lay, but most of them may almost certainly be ascribed to Phase IIg. There can be little, if any, doubt that the 'Great Treasure' and eight smaller deposits, which were all found in the 'burnt layer' in or about Schliemann's 'House of the City King', were left behind when the owners fled.

Many and varied objects were contained in these treasures. Ten of the deposits were largely made up of jewellery and ornaments obviously worn by women; three consisted mainly of men's weapons and gear; and three yielded a mixture of weapons, jewellery, and household utensils.

Schliemann's 'Great Treasure' was of this mixed kind. It included three vessels (among them a remarkable double sauceboat), two magnificent diadems, one plain narrow band, four elaborate basket-shaped ear-ornaments, 56 coils, perhaps

Plates 23, 24

74

hair-fasteners, six bracelets, and 8,700 beads of various sizes and shapes, all of gold; one goblet of electrum; six tongue-shaped bars, four tankards, two saucers, a shallow bowl, a goblet, two bottle-shaped vessels, and a small lid, all of silver; three large vessels (a basin, a pan, and a bucket), 20 blades of daggers or spears, three chisels, a knife, 14 flat celts, a damaged blade of a saw, and a fragment of a utensil of unknown use, all of copper or bronze.

The jewellery (all found in a large silver tankard, which contained also a fluted cup of electrum and one of gold) shows delicate, skilful workmanship: some pieces were cut out from thin gold sheets, others hammered out; wire was beaten out or drawn, and ornaments were attached as inlays or by soldering; patterns were executed in repoussé or granulated techniques. The designs are often simple, but occasionally, as in the diadem, they are relatively complex.

The principal diadem, as described by Schmidt, has at the top a fine horizontal chain, approximately 0.50 m. long; from this are suspended 90 chains of two different lengths, on which are strung small scale-like leaves. The eight outermost chains at each side are almost 0.38 m. long, each one terminating at the bottom in an attached idol-shaped pendant. The 74 intermediate chains are only 10 cm. long and end in two-pointed leaf-shaped figures. The chains themselves are formed by fine, separate, interlocking rings hammered out from four-sided wire. The leaves and pendants, cut from thin sheeting or gold leaf, have raised ribs in repoussé work; and the idol-like pendants are decorated with rows of punctated dots and with diminutive bosses or knobs.

The second necklace, of the same general type as the foregoing, though differing in details, is somewhat smaller, but equally elaborate in its construction. The four ear-rings, too, fashioned with comparable intricate designs, are small masterpieces of the goldsmith's art.

Plate 24

Another cache, Treasure D, found in a broken pot, comprised 16 coils, or hair-fasteners, four ear-rings, four large spacer beads, each in the form of quadruple spirals, two pins, each with a pair of spiral coils at the head, one pin with a ball at the top of the head, and six strings of beads of various shapes and sizes, all of gold; two bracelets and a pin of electrum; 11 coils (hair-fasteners), 20 parts of necklaces made of annular beads stuck together, 158 separate beads of the same kind, and remains of several further necklaces, all of silver.

It is clear from the objects found in these treasures that the women of the period – at least those of high social standing – were richly provided with costly ornaments and jewellery, and must have led a life of relative luxury. The great diadems and the corresponding ear-rings can only have belonged to court ladies accustomed to wealth and a lofty position. The royal family and its entourage were surely familiar with pomp and ceremony, and women evidently enjoyed a status of respect and standing.

Treasure L, discovered near the centre of the citadel in 1890, contained objects chiefly for men. They include four magnificent battle-axes, three of greenish stone said to be nephrite, and one of bluish stone resembling lapis lazuli, six hemispherical pommels of rock crystal (possibly three pairs), one pommel of ferruginous stone, 42 small pieces of rock crystal, each a segment of a sphere, polished on its upper surface, two almond-shaped pieces of rock crystal, plano-convex in shape, one of them ground on all sides, and two segments of the same shape.

Plate 25

The battle-axes are highly polished weapons of elegant form: around the middle, where there is a socket for the attachment of a handle, they are decorated in relief with delicately carved ridges and knobs, the interspaces between the ridges on two examples being filled with fine simple hatching. There can be no doubt that these are royal arms and they were surely made in the same atelier. The stone is not native in the Troad and the material must have been imported from abroad. Whether the workmanship was local or foreign has not been determined. The closest parallels have been found in Bessarabia. The crystal pommels probably served as heads for sceptres, or swords, or daggers, if they were not attached to the handles of the hammer-axes. The small segments of rock crystal were perhaps used as counters in a royal game, or may have been utilised as inlays.

Two small delicately worked lion-heads in rock crystal, which were found in house deposits and not in treasures, deserve particular mention. They were almost surely carved as knobs for light staffs or sceptres.

Plate 26

Among the metal (copper or bronze) weapons found in the great treasure and in some others, as well as generally in the layer of Troy II, there is no certain example of a long sword. The type may have existed, and it might appear if a cemetery of the period is ever discovered.

Many daggers – or spearheads (they are difficult to differentiate) – are in the Schliemann Collection and several different types are represented. Some examples show a relatively narrow leaf-shaped blade, drawn out at the hilt in a long, almost wire-like projection, usually bent at the end. The blade is pierced by a pair of longish slits or gashes through which the shaft, or handle, was presumably fastened by means of wire or thongs. A similar technique is illustrated by some spearheads found in Early Cycladic tombs. A second type of blade has rounded or angular shoulders and a short projecting tang, pierced by one or two rivet-holes for the attachment of the handle. A different kind of tanged dagger has its blade reinforced by a more or less conspicuous longitudinal midrib. In one of the most notable examples of this kind the relatively long, four-sided tang for the reception of a wooden or ivory grip is surmounted by the figure of a bull with spreading horns. Moulds of stone and possibly of terracotta for casting leaf-shaped blades and long narrow-bladed stilettos have likewise been recovered in deposits of Troy II – clear evidence for local manufacture. Primitive open one-piece, as well as two-piece, moulds occur.

Also to be counted among weapons are the fairly long, thin 'flat celts' of bronze or copper, some 30 of which were found by Schliemann. With a long handle attached about their middle they would serve usefully as battle-axes or hatchets. Several moulds of stone indicate that they were locally made. Arrowheads too are represented by plain, unbarbed darts, usually rectangular in section; they were drawn out with a shank to be fitted into the wooden shaft.

Copper and bronze knives have been recovered in consider-able numbers. Some are plain, with a single cutting edge, a few are double-edged. There are several of a distinctive type with the pointed end turned up sharply into a hook, sometimes almost like a spiraliform loop. At least one such knife is said by Schliemann to have been found in a stratum of Troy I, and an equally early example is known from the excavations of Miss Lamb at Thermi in Mitylene. Knives could be employed both as weapons and as implements. Chisels, drills, punches, pegs, and copper or bronze nails are also attested in some phases of Troy II.

Plate 26

We have cautiously referred to these metal objects as being made of copper or bronze. A few of the pieces found in Schliemann's 'treasures' have been properly analysed by pro-fessional metallurgists and have been identified as real bronzes. A good many fragments recovered from the habitation-debris, which have also been examined, have proved to be of copper with little or no tin. The general use of real bronze seems not to prevail until the time of Troy V, towards the end of the Early Bronze Age. The appearance of real bronze among the weapons found by Schliemann in his 'treasures' at a time when household articles were still being made for the most part of natural copper might perhaps signify that the latter were of domestic manufacture, while the daggers and spears of the ruler and nobles were imports from some foreign region metallurgically more advanced than the Troad.

The small drinking cups of gold and electrum, the goblets of silver as well as the bowls and saucers of silver and bronze, as found in the 'treasures', were no doubt made for practical use in wealthy households, if not in daily service, at least on occasions of state. The capacious bronze and copper vessels for storage and pouring of liquids, and the large pans and basins, were presumably likewise utilitarian accessories. The small gold and silver 'bottles' may have stood as ornaments or containers on the dressing-tables of the ladies. It is, however, difficult to imagine for what useful domestic purpose the curious double sauceboat of gold included in the 'Great Treasure' could have been designed. For want of a better explanation one may conjecture that it played some special rôle in ritual ceremonies. It has in any event a foreign shape and certainly points to connections with the Aegean or the Greek mainland.

Plate 23

For ordinary day-by-day household use in the preparation, service and storage of food, pottery made of clay was universally employed. A vast quantity of it has been recovered, by far the greater part in Schliemann's excavations. The circumstances of discovery, as recorded by him, are only in rare instances sufficiently detailed to make it clear to which specific layer of the Early Bronze Age it must be assigned. Indeed the greater part of Schliemann's ceramic collection could not be accurately arranged in its original stratigraphic order. Schmidt, who drew up the catalogue, was obliged to classify the wares largely on the evidence of style; and in dealing with his various categories he exercised caution and usually refrained from going beyond a general attribution to the whole succession of periods from Troy II to V inclusive. The excavations conducted by the Cincinnati Expedition have now given a certified sequence of pottery, not only for the major periods, but from virtually all

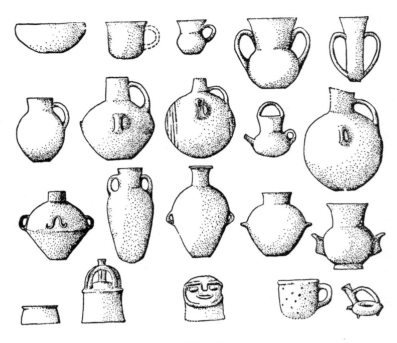

Fig. 19 Characteristic pottery shapes of Troy II

the component strata representing phases. This collection, too, is a fairly large one, comprising several hundred pots intact or reconstructed, and many thousands of fragments. Some 65 different shapes have been recognised in the material from Troy II, but they can by no means be taken as constituting the entire repertory; for many other forms of the less common types are doubtless represented by fragments too scanty or too small to permit restoration.

A survey of this material reveals that slow change and development marked the work done by the potters of Troy II. Beginning with the methods and traditions evolved and be-queathed by their predecessors of Troy I, and without appre-

Fig. 19

ciable outside influence, they produced through Phases IIa and IIb handmade Grey and Black Polished and Coarse Polished Wares, as well as a small quantity of red and black Lustre Ware, all practically indistinguishable from the corresponding fabrics of the First Settlement. But in Phase IIb a revolutionary innovation appears, which had a lasting influence on the subsequent history of pottery-making at Troy. This was the introduction or invention – one cannot yet say which – of the potter's wheel.

It did not instantly prevail and displace the old hand technique; that still survived through many phases alongside the new. But the effect of the wheel is to be seen in Phase IIc in a greatly increased production of plain flaring bowls, which exhibit clear marks of rotation, and it probably stimulated the potters generally and not merely in creating new shapes. Among the latter especially worth mentioning are heavy shallow dishes or plates of impressive size, smoothly finished, coated with a thick red or reddish wash and polished. They occur in abundance, both hand-made and wheel-made; and Schliemann, who found vast heaps of fragments, suggested that they may have been used as medallions to form friezes running around the walls of rooms. Equally noteworthy are the slender cylindrical two-handled goblets of a distinctive Trojan form, with a heart-shaped contour, familiar to archaeologists under the name *depas amphikypellon*, a term which was taken from the *Iliad* by Schliemann and applied to these cups when he thought the 'Burnt City' was Homeric Troy. A much more capacious one- or two-handled goblet or tankard is also characteristic of the period, and its size inclines one toward a wholesome respect for Trojan drinking habits of this time.

There are several other shapes of pots evidently of Trojan invention that cannot be passed over without mention, even in a very brief survey of this pottery: large ovoid jugs and flasks; clumsy feeding bottles with globular body, high neck, basket

Plate 27

Fig. 19

Plate 27

handle, and a tubular spout projecting from the lower part of the side; large globular or ovoid jars with high collar-like neck, which often bears a conventionalised representation of human features – eyes, nose, ears in relief and occasionally also the mouth. Sometimes this decoration was placed not on the neck, but on a neatly adjusted cylindrical lid that fitted closely over it. The lid is usually disk-like, flat or rounded on its upper surface, and surmounted by an ornamental tassel or knob. This custom of decorating pots with plastic representations of the human face is of course a direct inheritance from Troy I, a ceramic reflection of a style of sculpture that had already been evolved in stone.

The pottery made and used in the time of Troy II was still, as in the preceding period, predominantly monochrome. Painted decoration is almost non-existent, being represented only by two or three small sherds, possibly from imported vessels. No real attempt seems to have been made to variegate the appearance of the ordinary household pots and pans of the day by the use of bright contrasting colours. They show almost invariably a more or less uniform – not to say monotonous – single colour, black, grey, or red. One can hardly avoid concluding that the Trojans of this age were a dour, austere people, with little fondness for gaiety and light. The general heaviness of the pottery, except for the scanty Lustre Ware, offers a striking contrast to the delicacy of the jewellery found in the same stratum. Perhaps the goldsmith's art was more advanced than the potter's. Not that decorated pottery was unknown or even uncommon: for many vases carry striking and effective designs executed in grooved and incised techniques, or in raised relief. But in the latter, at least, the style is relatively heavy, lacking in lightness of touch. This quality is well illustrated in the faces on lids and necks of jars: the features are severe and stern, modelled by a ponderous hand, with scanty concessions to geniality and good humour.

A developed feeling for decorative art is recognisable in the numerous incised or impressed white-filled motifs that appear in hundreds, if not thousands, of terracotta whorls, which constitute one of the most distinctive products of Trojan handicrafts. In the realm of the major arts there is little surviving evidence. Sculpture in stone comparable to the carved stele of Troy I has not been found. Remains of frescoes or wall-paintings of any kind are likewise still lacking. But in the ruins of the *megara* as well as in the fortifications, we see that architecture had risen to a high stage of achievement. Orderly plans, carefully aligned and well-built walls, trimly worked stone parastade-bases and column-bases all reveal a collabora-tion of architects and artisans who had behind them traditions, training and experience which had no doubt established cer-tain standards. The level reached in this branch of art gives ground for believing that there must have been corresponding progress in the other major fields.

Not to be classed among important artistic products, but interesting in itself, is a crude and careless sketch which was incised lightly on the exterior of a thick red plate, or on a large fragment of such a plate that was already broken. It is a childish drawing, in fine lines scratched by a sharp point, showing the upper part of an armed warrior, with head in profile, shoulders in frontal view. He seems to be wearing a tight-fitting crested helmet. The bird-like face is formed by two sharp projecting angles which might be meant to suggest nose and chin. The head is small, supported on an enormously long thin neck. From broad shoulders the body tapers to a narrow waist. Over the right shoulder hangs a sash that passes diagon-ally across the chest to the left side; something was suspended from it, perhaps a quiver or some kind of a weapon. The left arm is bent at the elbow and seems to have held a flag or pennant attached to a staff. The right arm is raised high and drawn back as if about to throw a spear or other missile. A

Fig. 16

Plate 27

horizontal line at the waist with the suggestion of a fring
below it may mark the bottom of a leather cuirass. This simpl
sketch on a sherd from the stratum of Troy IIc gives us the onl
contemporary drawing we have of a human figure.

The objects recovered from the debris of the Second Settle
ment shed little light on the religious life of the community
Indeed, apart from great numbers of the familiar idols of ston
and bone, there is nothing that can surely be interpreted a
having to do with cults. The Schliemann Collection con
tained 409 idols of stone, chiefly marble, one of shell, 27 o
bone, and eight of terracotta, a grand total of 445. How man

Plate 26

of these are assignable to Troy II is uncertain, but almost al
may safely be attributed to the Early Bronze Age. The Cincin
nati Expedition recovered from the various strata of Troy I
nine idols of stone and 11 of bone, and for the Early Bronz
Age, including all categories, a total of 49 figures. In genera
there is almost no perceptible difference between the example
found in strata of Troy I and those from Troy II, and this als
applies when we compare the idols from Troy II with thos
of Settlements III, IV, and V. To the end of the Early Bronz
Age we thus seem to have a continuity of cult and culture
Götze regards these idols as amulets and charms that could b
carried for luck by individuals. Perhaps they were also kept a
'icons' in the home.

Schliemann reports that he discovered the skeleton of
woman in a house of the Second City. The house had bee
destroyed by fire, which apparently also caused the woman'
death. At all events, the skeleton was found in a strang
attitude, almost as if standing, clearly not as it would have bee
placed in a proper burial. Beside it were recovered several coil
of gold wire, perhaps hair-fasteners, a straight pin of electrum
and a number of small gold beads. In the southwestern par
of the citadel Schliemann came upon two male skeletons i
the debris of the Third City. As mentioned above, he believe

them to be the remains of two warriors who had perished in the fire. A jar unearthed by him in a deposit of the 'Burnt City' contained the skull of a young woman; and a smaller vessel from a contemporary context, half the skeleton of an embryo. Apart from the latter, these human remains seem not to represent normal burials.

Three graves were uncovered by the Cincinnati Expedition in the layer of Troy II inside the citadel. One of them, assignable to IIb or IIc, was that of an adult female, some 30 years old. The body, lying on its left side in a contracted position, had been deposited without accompanying objects in a small depression, which had been hollowed out in the fortification wall of Troy IIa and lined with small stone slabs set on edge. Another grave, attributed to Phase IIf, contained the skeleton of a child of about eight; it lay on its right side in contracted position in a small pit under a floor. There were no objects with it. The third burial was that of a child of 12 or 13; this body, too, had been placed in a flexed position on its right side in a shallow gravepit sunk beneath a floor of Phase IIg. The only accompanying object was a small bit of lead wire.

The rare occurrence of graves inside the settlement makes it clear that, except possibly in the case of children, it was not a regular custom in this period to bury the dead within the walls of the town. Schliemann's explorations outside the citadel in search of cemeteries, and the similar efforts of both Dörpfeld and the Cincinnati Expedition, have all been fruitless so far as the Early Bronze Age is concerned. Schliemann believed that cremation was practised in that period, but until further evidence becomes available we cannot be sure how the inhabitants of Troy II disposed of their dead. Contemporary cemeteries containing many graves have been discovered at Soma, Yortan, Balikesir, Bozüyük and Babaköy. There may be similar burials in the vicinity of Troy, but, if so, they must be well concealed.

Plate 28

During the time of Troy II it is clear that the community was not isolated from the surrounding world: there certainly were relations with other regions, friendly or hostile, and in some way an exchange of products was effected. The substantial quantities of gold, silver, lead, copper, and bronze – found for the most part by Schliemann – are not of local origin, but must have been brought from outside sources. Obsidian came from Melos, and perhaps also marble from the Cyclades, for making idols and vessels. Nephrite and the lapis-like stone from which the royal battle-axes were made, as already stated, must have been imported from Bessarabia or some more remote region. While raw materials were no doubt acquired for the purpose of manufacturing locally many objects such as the marble idols, in other instances, as for example the magnificent hammer-axes, and some pieces of the gold ornaments and jewellery, the finished products may have been imported. A stone pestle and silver tweezers are likely to have come already manufactured from the Cyclades; the double sauceboat of gold perhaps also arrived in a finished state, as well as some distinctive Cycladic tubes of bone for holding pigment.

Foreign pottery, which had begun to find its way into Troy I, was still coming into Troy II, and continued to do so through the rest of the Early Bronze Age. Most of it is of an Early Aegean type, Cycladic or Helladic, with characteristic pieces of monochrome glazed ware, predominantly red or reddish, sometimes black. Another distinctive variety, of hard compact fabric, with blue-grey core, smoothly finished and coated with a thin wash, light-red, tan or grey in colour, occurs frequently in large storage jars. The Cincinnati Expedition thought it might be a local kind of Cycladic glazed ware, but it could equally well come from some Aegean island. There is also a related, but not glazed, variety, almost surely produced by the local potters in imitation of the finer ware. This too appears mainly in tall capacious jars. Almost all of the vases that may be regarded as imports are ordinary pots for practical household use. Few if any have claims to artistic merit. Most of them are of considerable size and it is obvious that they were imported not for themselves but for their contents. Possibly they served as containers of olive oil that was being brought from the Aegean.

In what manner all these imported objects were acquired by the Trojans has not yet been established. Among historians, one school has long held that 'trade' and 'commerce' in the Bronze Age are no more than polite terms for raiding and looting. Certainly such a system of exchange survived to the end of the Late Bronze Age and beyond, as we know from the Homeric poems. Gold, silver, bronze, and other articles of intrinsic value were no doubt carried off in many a piratical incursion; but small bowls, cups, jugs, and big pots of ordinary household crockery are unlikely to have been brought home in relatively great numbers as booty. In the present writer's opinion, therefore, some organised method of barter must be postulated even for the third millennium B C.

What, then, did the people of Troy have to give in exchange ? Trojan pottery - or imitations of it - has been found, especially as represented by the highly distinctive *depas*, in a remarkably widespread distribution ranging from central Anatolia, Cilicia, and northern Syria to the Cyclades, the Greek mainland, and on the north to Thrace and even to southeastern Bulgaria. In many instances, as Bittel has shown, there is no question of real identity with the Trojan wares, and local production is probable; but in other instances the resemblance is so close that a connection is virtually certain. The broad chronological span over which the *depas* - with little perceptible change - was made and used at Troy is far too great to permit precise synchronisms; but one cannot avoid the conclusion that this distribution of the *depas* betokens extensive Trojan influence. Elegant small cups of this kind were certainly not shipped so far away for their contents; they must in themselves have become desirable objects of trade.

But pottery alone would not have sufficed to bring a large influx of gold into Troy. Agricultural products may have contributed something. The animal bones found in the excavations show that the town possessed an abundance of live stock, especially cattle, sheep and goats, for which there may have been a good market. And surely there must have been a substantial production of wool for which one can readily imagine a steady demand in the islands of the Aegean. It is not unlikely that the Trojans also manufactured and exported woollen textiles, even on a scale that would bring in an appreciable equivalent in gold. The multitude of terracotta whorls or buttons, some 8,000 to 10,000 of which were recovered by Schliemann, seem to indicate a special interest in clothing made of heavy fabrics. Moreover, one may conjecture that enterprising rulers of the Troad did not fail to exploit the forests that must have covered the foothills that ascend toward Mount Ida. Timber for building boats and ships, and for the wooden framework of houses made of stone and crude brick must always have been wanted in the nearly treeless Cyclades. Lumber, textiles, and wool, all are perishable materials that would have been consumed by time, leaving few if any recognisable traces. Only the scattered remains of Trojan cups and jars have survived here and there to shed a little light on what was probably once a lively traffic by ships that rollowed routes across the Aegean to the islands and the mainland of Greece and along the Anatolian coast southward and eastward to Cilicia and Syria.

If still more is needed to explain the prosperity of the Second Settlement I think we must bear in mind the possibility already mentioned, that the kings of Troy were able to levy tolls on all those who passed with their goods, by water or by land, through Trojan territory.

The actual source of the gold contained in Schliemann's treasures has not been specifically determined. Strabo states that there were once gold mines in the Troad. Not very far away in Lydia is the river Pactolus, famous for its golden sands; and gold may likewise have come from Phrygia. Whatever the specific place of origin of all this gold found at Troy, its accumulation must have been the product of management and toil spread over a long time. The king and his advisers were no doubt the capitalists who controlled economic enterprises, and the profits were presumably theirs.

The fire that destroyed the entire establishment, bringing Troy IIg to its end, was evidently a great disaster, wrecking Trojan prosperity. The survivors were, however, able to rebuild the whole town and to initiate a long era of recovery that lasted through Troy III, IV, and V, to the end of the Early Bronze Age. The archaeological evidence indicates that there was no break in cultural continuity, no sign of any fresh influence from outside the Troad. On the contrary, the reconstructed Troy seems to have been occupied by the same people, who followed the same way of life and clung to the same traditions as their immediate predecessors. The miscellaneous objects of copper and bronze which they have left us, their implements, tools and figures of stone and bone, their whorls of terracotta, and their pottery – all display a continuing evolution of ideas and types bequeathed by ancestors on the site.

This power of tenacious survival on the inherited ground is perhaps one of the most striking characteristics of the people who flourished on the Trojan acropolis through the Early Bronze Age. Their roots, as we have noted, go down to the very beginning of that era, and indeed there is some basis for the presumption that they may have sprung from still older origins in the neolithic levels at Kum Tepe. Despite the disastrous conflagration that swept over the whole settlement, leaving ruin in its wake to mark the end of Troy II, and other

similar catastrophes that struck from time to time, these earl
Trojans, as we shall see, continued through many furthe
centuries, in Troy III, IV and V, to hold their commandin
position in the Troad. So long a domination, apparently un
troubled by explosive internal disorders and undisturbed b
hostile attacks from abroad, means that a general state of peac
prevailed or was maintained; and we may with considerabl
assurance conclude that a stable government existed and exer
cised control over an efficient system of administration.

CHAPTER V

The Early Bronze Age: Troy III to V

THE WORK OF the Cincinnati Expedition has shown that the Third, Fourth, and Fifth Settlements, though not of the greatest importance, were somewhat more than 'miserable villages', as Dörpfeld characterised them. Each seems to have had a fortification wall; each apparently occupied a somewhat larger area and had a greater population than its predecessor. In each period, houses, laid out in irregular blocks separated by narrow streets, evidently filled all the area within the defensive walls. Each presumably continued to be the seat of a ruler or king, though no remains of an actual palace have survived. The central part of the citadel, where the royal residence might be expected to have stood, was dug away by Schliemann who removed all the walls without recording them in great detail. He does, however, mention a building of considerable size that was demolished in order to expose the underlying *Megaron* II A, and it may well have been the palace of Troy III.

TROY III

In the areas examined by the most recent excavators the Third Settlement was found to be represented by a stratified deposit ranging in thickness from 2 to 2.65 m.; in some places it was made up of three strata, in others of four, obviously correspond, ing to an equal number of phases. Some of the house walls from the beginning of the period exhibited a peculiarity that marked them out from the similar structures in all other early periods at Troy: the whole wall, all the way to its top, was built of stone, whereas in earlier and later times it was custom, ary to erect only a low socle of stone, 0.30 to 0.60 m. high, which supported a superstructure of crude brick. Perhaps the

Plate 29

ruins of Troy II provided on the spot so great an abundance of ready-to-hand building material of stone that it was simpler and more economical to use it rather than to bring in clay to make bricks. In any event, stone walls more than 2 m. high were still standing in buildings of Troy III. In the later phases of Troy III walls were occasionally made of alternating horizontal bands of stonework and brickwork, a system that had already been used in some phases of Troy II.

Separate free-standing houses were apparently rare – if they occurred at all. Ordinary people evidently lived in apartments of one, two, or three rooms contained in a larger structure and separated by party walls, each division provided with a door way that opened on a street, and there may have been unroofed courts of no great size. Walls were normally coated with rough mud plaster, sometimes finished with a final wash of clay Floors were made of clay, and small areas of irregular shape baked hard by fire, had served as hearths.

Fig. 20

Until recently few if any objects in the Schliemann Collection could with absolute certainty be attributed to the Third Settlement. Now a good deal of certified material has become available; for the Cincinnati Expedition recovered from un-disturbed deposits some 445 miscellaneous items of metal stone, bone, shell, and terracotta, and was able to put together or restore 195 pots of various sizes and shapes, besides assembling a large collection of potsherds. Although this material might seem like skimmed milk in comparison with the rich cream that Schliemann must have collected, it does give us authentic evidence regarding the character of Troy III.

Among the 22 copper pins that were brought to light, one, with a head formed of wire loops, is of distinctively Cycladic type, though other similar pieces have a widely scattered dis tribution. All the rest find parallels not only in Troy I and II but in central Anatolia as well as in the Aegean region. Four needles, with slit-like eye-hole well down on the shaft, recall

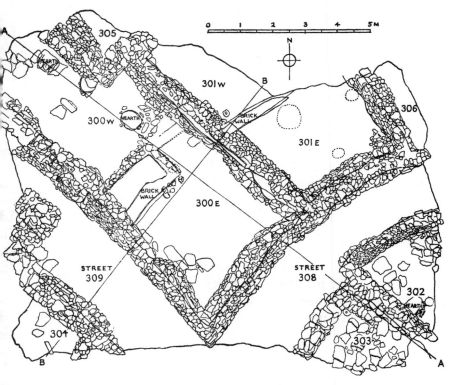

Fig. 20 Plan of houses of Troy III in Square E 6

cal ancestors of Troy I. A fragment of a knife blade, up⁄
ɪrved at the pointed end, also probably has antecedents in the
ɪrst Settlement, and has at least one analogy from an Early
.elladic house at Eutresis in Boeotia. Comparable curving
ɪives much later were used by the Hittites in central Asia
ɪinor.

Included among the 102 stone objects from undisturbed
ɪposits are three flakes of obsidian, no doubt of Melian origin,
ong with 20 idols almost all of marble and of several types;

Plate 30

93

forerunners of these latter may be recognised in Troy I and I
They are for the most part simple versions of the famili
fiddle-shaped figures from the Cyclades. One limestone id
from Troy III and another of the same material, but of uncertai
stratigraphic provenience, are exceptionally big, the form
being 0.35 m., the latter, lacking its head, 0.45 m. high. A
head such as No. 7597 in the Schliemann Collection, abov
0.20 m. high, would make the total height of the figure uj
wards of 0.65 m. Such ponderous pieces could not be amule
or talismans to be carried in a pocket; they must have stood i
fixed positions in a house or a shrine.

Plate 30

Objects of bone, totalling 100, include 86 awls and pins o
seven or eight different types, most of which are familiar
Early Aegean and Anatolian sites. Somewhat more notab
are four flat idols, resembling those of marble; there are al
four small tubes, which usually bear incised decoration; th
may have been used as handles for knives or daggers or impl
ments. One tube found by Schliemann is almost surely
Cycladic original which once served as a container for pi;
ments – perhaps for make-up or tattooing. Two or three car
fully worked ornaments, possibly parts of head-bands o
diadems, deserve special mention; they are neatly decorate
with incised dotted circles, generally arranged in rows clo
together. A curious item, apparently *sui generis*, is a large se
tion of the horn of a deer or a mountain goat, one end of whic
has been roughly and only partly carved to represent a huma
head. It might possibly have been intended for a handle or
grip of some heavy weapon or implement.

The material itself is of some interest, for an examination b
a zoologist, N. Gejvall, of the animal bones collected from th
debris of Troy III revealed that, in comparison with Troy
and II, there had been a spectacular increase in the inciden
of bones of *cervus dama*. Venison had now become the mo
popular kind of meat, followed by mutton, pork, and beef

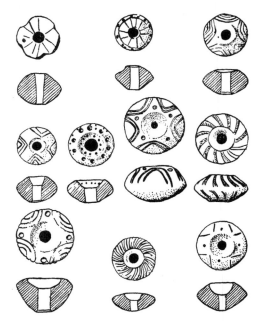

at order. The rather abrupt appearance of deer in appreciably
reater numbers than heretofore must presumably mean that
ew methods of hunting had been developed; it might be an
dvance in skill or technique, the acquisition of better deer
ounds, or the invention of more effective weapons, although
ne cannot leave out of account the possibility of climatic
nanges favouring the expansion of pasturage for wild deer.

Whorls to the number of 177 make up the bulk of the 209
ems of terracotta catalogued by the Cincinnati Expedition.
1 shape and decoration they differ very little from their fore-
nners of Troy II. We may regard as innovations, on the
her hand, two crudely fashioned quadrupeds; fragments of
vo or three others indicate that such figures were not rare.
chliemann, who found a good many, states that they turned

Fig. 21

up only in what he called the 'Fourth City' (which is in part a
least to be equated with our Troy III). Some of these creature
appear to be dogs, others may represent sheep or cattle, bu
they are modelled so carelessly that one cannot be sure. In othe
regions comparable animal figures occur freely in deposits c
the Copper Age and Early Bronze Age both in Anatolia an
in the Aegean, but local distinctive types are not easily di
tinguishable. Among the terracottas it may be worth notin
from Troy III a single brush-handle; except that it is mucl
more neatly made, it takes its place in a series beginning i
Troy II and continuing into Troy IV.

Fig. 22

Considered as a whole, the pottery of Troy III is practicall
indistinguishable from that of Troy II. With insignificar
omissions the same wares continue to appear in roughly th

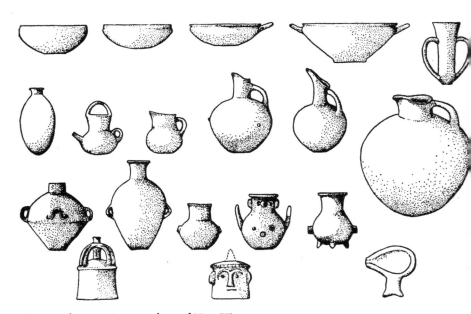

Fig. 22 Characteristic pottery shapes of Troy III

ame proportions. Most of the shapes that were popular in the
econd Settlement still enjoy favour in equal measure in the
'hird. Some small differences may, however, be noted: several
napes that were fairly common in Troy II have not been
:cognised in Troy III, and conversely, in the latter a few new
orms emerge. Since most of these occur only infrequently, the
ailure to notice them in the material of Troy II might be to
ome extent fortuitous. Still, these and other minor differences,
·hen added together, indicate that the ceramic industry was
ot unaffected by changing conditions, needs, and demands.
'he flaring bowl, which is present in vast numbers, be
omes somewhat thicker, deeper, and larger than in Troy II.
t the same time a slight alteration in the quality of the slip
id the manner of polishing is to be observed in Red-coated
Vare.

In general, flaring bowls, deeper bowls with rounded shoul
er, one-handled tankards, the tall slender *depas amphikypellon*
ith its two handles, large jugs with cylindrical neck and
orizontal lip, spouted jugs, beaked jugs, face-pots and lids, **Plate 31,**
iree-legged jars, and baking dishes are among the most dis **Fig. 23**
nctive products turned out by the potters of Troy III. Along
de these local wares through all phases of the period there is
constant, though not abundant, accompaniment of pottery
·idently imported from Early Cycladic and Early Helladic
:ntres. Almost all the vessels represented are fairly large, and
is likely that they were brought to Troy filled with some
ommodity such as olive oil.

Among the best of the local Trojan vases not a few, despite
teir monochrome technique, stand out as pleasing, attractive
·eations in the ceramic field. Otherwise little has been recov
ed from the ruins of Troy III that can support any serious
aim to consideration for its artistic value. The two fragment **Plate 30**
y 'diadems' and a decorative strip, all made of deer horn,
iow delicate and skilful workmanship; nor are the decorated

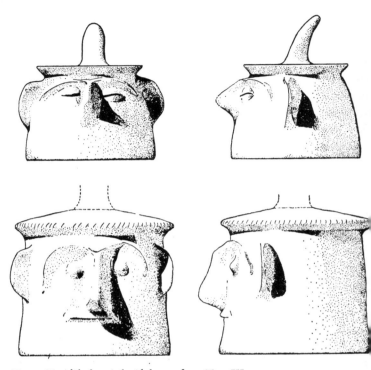

Fig. 23 Two lids decorated with human faces, Troy III

whorls without style and charm. The face-pots, too, seem t
show an increased facility on the part of the potters; an im
provement is to be noticed especially in the more huma
quality they manage to impart to their subjects. But the terra
cotta figures of animals are distinguished mainly by the
crudity, and no more can be said for the human face carved a
one end of a deer-horn. The absence of any notable works c
art does not necessarily mean that none ever existed; where s
much has been lost, negative evidence is not decisive. But Tro
III could probably boast few artists of distinction.

After passing through three phases or more, Troy III came to its end. How this was brought about is not clear. One house was certainly wrecked by fire, but there seems to have been no continuous layer of burned debris to indicate that the whole settlement perished in a general conflagration. On the other hand there can be no doubt that all the houses in the citadel were destroyed, and a new town was built over the ruins of the old one.

The new establishment, Troy IV, stretching out over and beyond the ruins of the Third Settlement, occupied an expanse of some 17,000 or more square metres, or approximately four acres. The remains of the Fourth Settlement were dug away by Schliemann, throughout the greater part of the acropolis: in consequence, only relatively small remnants of undisturbed deposit were available for examination in the most recent excavations and the material recovered is correspondingly meagre. The places that could be tested were, however, widely scattered, one in the middle of the citadel, another in the eastern quarter, a third on the southern slope, and two others toward the southwest and at the western end of the hill; the net yield of evidence may, therefore, safely be taken as representative. The depth of the layer varied generally from 1.70 to 2 m. and more; but near the eastern edge there was a massive accumulation of debris more than 5 m. thick. This latter unfortunately could not be investigated in detail, for it lay directly beneath House VI F, one of the important buildings of the Sixth Settlement, the destruction of which was not to be contemplated. The layer was everywhere seen to be composed of successive strata: in the key areas a sequence of five phases was thus definitely established. For convenience they have been called IVa, IVb, and so on to IVe. No appreciable difference from one to another could be discerned, but taken togethe they must indicate a period of some duration.

Observations along the eastern and southern borders of th settlement led to the conclusion that the citadel – on these side at least – was surrounded by a substantial wall of stones; it ma have served a double purpose, as a support for a high towr terrace along the outer edge and also as a defensive worl Lying deeply buried beneath later buildings and debris, th wall has been seen only in short sections of one face or th other; its original thickness is unknown and details of i construction have not been ascertained. None the less it give ground for assuming that Troy IV still maintained its characte as a stronghold.

The town itself, like its immediate predecessor, consisted c houses standing contiguously, one beside another, and formin smallish complexes, or 'squares', of casual shapes and irregula sizes, separated by winding lanes. In alignment neither th streets nor the blocks of houses correspond at all closely wit those they displaced. The foundations of the new houses seer to have been laid out without reference to the underlying wal of Troy III, which were covered by debris and no longe visible. It is worth noting that the masons who worked on th programme of rebuilding turned back in their technique to th old style of construction that prevailed in Troy II and earlie when only a low socle or podium was made of stone while th actual wall it supported was built of crude brick. As in th preceding periods, all wall faces seem to have been coated wit a thick plaster of mud or clay.

The appearance of what seems to be a new house plan deserves attention. It is a fairly large building which containe at least four separate dwellings, side by side, divided from on another by party walls, and each, consisting of one or tw rooms, opening on the same street. It might almost be called tenement house; and perhaps it would not be too rash to cor

Fig. 24

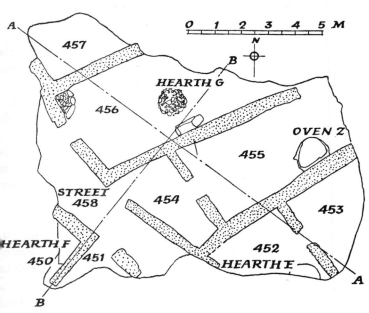

Fig. 24 Plan of houses, Phase IVa, in Square E 6

lude that the population of the town had increased, possibly
accompanied by a decline in prosperity. For these are obviously
not the homes of wealthy citizens.

Another novel feature in Troy IV is the sudden introduction, in Phase IVa, of a domed oven. It evidently soon became
popular, for in the restricted area examined by the Cincinnati
Expedition remains of five or six comparable structures were
brought to light. In at least one instance the oven was set up
indoors, inside a house; but sometimes – perhaps more often –
it may have stood out of doors in an unroofed court. The invention and installation of what looks like a good oven might be
interpreted as pointing to a rise in the standard of living. If the
people of Troy III – as we were tempted to conjecture – ate a
good deal more than their ancestors of the Second Settlement,

perhaps we are justified in concluding that their descendant of Troy IV gave more attention to cooking and the preparation of food. Their meat diet – on the evidence of the animal bone collected – was of considerable variety, including venison pork, mutton and goat, beef and rabbit, in that order of prefer ence or use. One household apparently had a special fondnes for turtle steak or soup, and almost all seem to have enjoye sea food.

As in Troy III, the bones of deer continue to be abundan in the Fourth Settlement, and, in comparison with those o other animals, such bones are frequently used as material fo making implements. A crude sketch of a stag with hug antlers which was carelessly incised to decorate the top of cylindrical flanged lid of pottery, may perhaps be regarded a further evidence of the important rôle played by deer.

Miscellaneous objects that may with certainty be attribute to Troy IV number only some 232; these were found in th most recent excavations. The 11 scanty bits of copper o bronze comprise seven wire pins, one needle, an awl or dar and two flat, shaped pieces that bear some resemblance t primitive figurines or idols; two similar objects in the Schlie mann Collection have been explained as razors, and there ar two comparable pieces with long blades which must surely b knives.

Stone objects of certified stratigraphic provenience, totallin 69, include eight flat idols of types familiar from earlier layers two bits of obsidian, 17 flint blades, and some other weapon and implements, but there is nothing of quality or distinction The bone objects, 39 in number, are equally insignificant s far as shedding any new light on the culture of Troy IV i concerned; and the same judgment must be passed on most o the 111 objects of terracotta. But the whorls, which total 92 and obviously carry on the old local tradition, are of som interest, since more than two-thirds of them are decorated wit

Plate 32

Plate 33

Fig. 25

incised – and once white-filled – patterns. This is a greater proportionate incidence of decoration on whorls than has been observed in any other period. Does it perhaps mean that the inhabitants of the Fourth Settlement were much more interested in decorative art than would be suggested by a first glance at the scanty and unexciting remains that chance has allowed to survive?

The pottery of Troy IV, which holds fast to the ceramic methods and traditions of the past on the site, requires only a brief survey. A study of large quantities of fragmentary material and the 110 or more pots that came from certified contexts in the successive strata reveals evidence of gradual development, but no great or abrupt changes. Some 59 different shapes could be

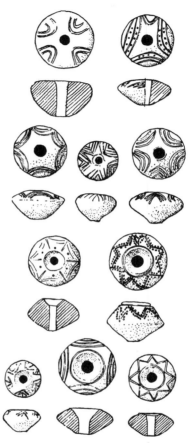

Fig. 25 Decorated whorls of Troy IV

recognised. The use of straw-tempering in making large vessels – which had already been tried in Troy III – is now generally adopted. The potter's wheel, too, is employed much more freely than before, though hand-made articles still appear. Most of the ordinary pottery was rather carelessly made for practical use, but in some instances vases seemed to have been

Fig. 26

Plate 32

designed with a view to artistic effect. Among them are large jars with wing-like attachments on the sides and applied plastic decoration in broadly curving spiraliform strips. Painted patterns are relatively rare, and are limited chiefly to simple large crosses on the interiors or bottoms of shallow bowls. One-handled and two-handled cups are popular, face-pots and lids continue to be made and used, as well as the *depas amphikypellon*, though not so frequently as in Troy III.

No graves of the Fourth Settlement have been discovered, and nothing is known about the burial customs of the period.

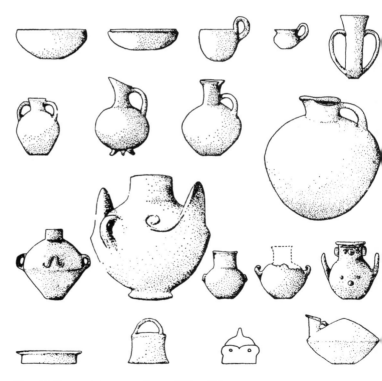

Fig. 26 Characteristic pottery shapes of Troy IV

The Cincinnati Expedition did, however, find itself confronted by an unsolved mystery: in a stratum of Phase IVe (in Square F 8) a lone adult human skull came to light, unaccompanied by other bones. A search in the neighbourhood failed to reveal any clue as to how it came to be there. Was this perhaps the carelessly discarded head of some unfortunate dismembered victim slain in the final destruction of the settlement? We should very much like to know, since there is no clear evidence to explain how Troy IV came to its end.

The Fifth Settlement has left ruins and heaped-up rubbish that formed a layer with an average thickness of at least 1.50 m. Widely spread representative deposits overlying those of Troy IV were investigated by the Cincinnati Expedition in the central, eastern, southern, southwestern, and western parts of the acropolis. In all these areas the accumulation was seen to be composed of distinctly marked strata of habitation wreckage and rubbish, accounting for a sequence of three or four chronological phases. It is not certain that the layer was complete in all the places tested; in some, at any rate, the topmost stratum had apparently suffered considerable damage as a result of later intrusions from above.

The period begins with a general rebuilding of the whole town. For a start the Trojans are likely to have built a fortification wall that perhaps – like its predecessor in Troy IV – also held up a terrace at least along the southern and eastern flanks of the hill. The wall has not actually been seen, but, as demonstrated by the horizontal strata it once supported, it must have replaced or re-used parts of an earlier structure of the same kind that had served a similar purpose.

With their neat, relatively thin and light walls and, in some instances, their greater regularity of plan as compared with

those of the preceding period, the new houses display some
definite signs of improvement in the technique of building.
The comparatively spacious character of these new dwellings
suggests that the Fourth Settlement might well – before its

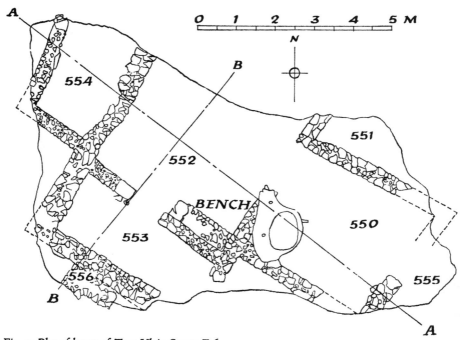

Fig. 27 Plan of houses of Troy Vb in Square E 6

end – have attained a state of considerable prosperity which
enabled the inhabitants to adopt an ambitious programme of
reconstruction when that became necessary. One representative
house now had a principal room at least 10 m. long and half
as wide, with connecting chambers on at least three sides.
Built-in furniture likewise makes its appearance; hearths and
Plate 34   domed ovens, first introduced in Troy IV, continue to be

standard equipment, while seats and benches made of clay –
which were also invented in the time of the Fourth Settlement –
are now constructed in a more finished style in corners of
rooms. One or two of the beehive ovens are elaborately designed
with neat fire-boxes underneath and flues leading upward.

Plate 35

As noted in the account of the earlier eras on the site, it looks
as if there was from period to period a steady, if slow, rise in
the standard of living. Certainly slight changes in manners,
customs, ideas, and even diet may be assumed as natural with
the passage of time. One innovation in Troy V – greatly to be
deplored from the archaeological point of view – was the
adoption of more effective methods of house-cleaning. The
floors were now to a great extent swept and kept clean of the
ordinary day-by-day accumulation of rubbish, and disappointingly little in the way of animal bones, miscellaneous objects,
discarded or lost, and whole or broken pottery was left on the
floor to be found by excavators. Some of the latter can hardly
be blamed for feeling a prejudice against the inhabitants of the
Fifth Settlement.

The animal bones recovered from certified strata, though not
over-abundant, seem to show an appreciable falling off in the
consumption of venison in the town; beef and pork, it would
appear, were the most favoured meat dishes on the menu of the
community.

The miscellaneous objects recovered from controlled stratified
areas are unfortunately too scanty to allow much in the way of
general conclusions. A few pieces of metal include a plain
knife, a chisel, three pins, and a bit of wire, all of bronze or
copper, and a rolled-up piece of thin lead strip. Some sample
fragments which have been analysed show that real bronze was
now being made and used in Troy V. The objects of stone
and bone offer almost nothing of any significance. The terracottas include a fragment of an animal figurine, recalling forerunners of the Third Settlement, a loom weight, ten pierced

Plate 36

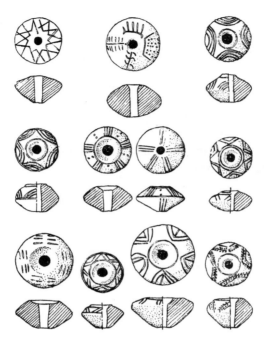

Fig. 28 Decorated whorls of Troy V

Fig. 28

disks cut from potsherds, and some 88 whorls of many different shapes, all familiar in preceding periods on the site. The proportional frequencies of the most popular types are virtually the same through the entire sequence of periods from Troy II to V inclusive; a clear demonstration of the continuity of culture through many centuries of apparently peaceful, untroubled occupation of this site.

Fig. 29

A survey of the pottery bears out this conclusion. Only 35 whole or nearly complete vessels were recovered from stratified deposits, but substantial quantities of contemporary potsherds provide abundant supplementary evidence. In the early phase of Troy V the wares and shapes that predominated in the Fourth Settlement are still characteristic. In the middle and

Plate 37

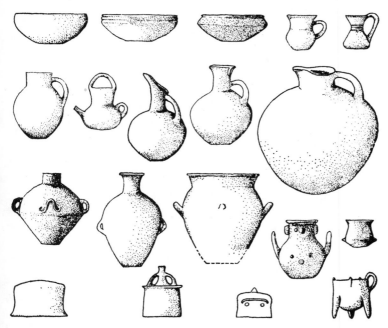

Fig. 29 Characteristic pottery shapes of Troy V

late phases one may observe a general advance in technical skill as well as in artistic expression. A few innovations in shapes, or in modifications of earlier types, also make their appearance. The pots are now more carefully formed and fired, with the result that greater symmetry of contour and a smoother surface finish, a more even quality and brighter colours in the glaze-like coating of the exterior are achieved. Shallow bowls decorated outside or inside with a broad painted cross occur frequently, continuing a mannerism first used in Troy IV. Incised decoration as well as the application of plastic ornament in the old manner are still employed by the potters, who occasionally also work out patterns in burnishing strokes.

Plate 37

A lone human bone (a right femur of a male) came to light in a stratum probably belonging to the initial phase of Troy V. In a deposit apparently assignable to Phase Vc an infant burial was discovered just beneath the floor of House 501. The skeleton, lying in a flexed position, was that of a new-born babe, and there were no accompanying objects. Similar interments of infants beneath floors of houses have been noted in earlier periods, the custom going back to Troy I. Real cemeteries of the Fifth Settlement have eluded discovery, despite extensive exploration, and nothing is known about burial customs.

Although the evidence is still lamentably meagre, one who has studied this material cannot help feeling that had the life of this town been extended by a half-century or a century, the Fifth Settlement would probably have evolved and created a notable and highly distinctive era of Early Bronze Age culture in its late blossoming. But this was not to be. In some manner, not yet explained, the town was again destroyed. The ruins showed no recognisable signs of a devastating fire, nothing to suggest an attack and capture by enemies with the use of force and violence. In the absence of evidence of that kind some archaeologists have been reluctant to accept the view that the end of Troy V marks a major break in continuity. But the houses were certainly demolished, whatever the manner, and in Troy VI a new town was erected, a town which in its buildings seems to have followed a wholly independent plan that took no account of walls of houses and streets that had gone before.

1

8   9

11

14

17

18

19

20

21

22

23

24

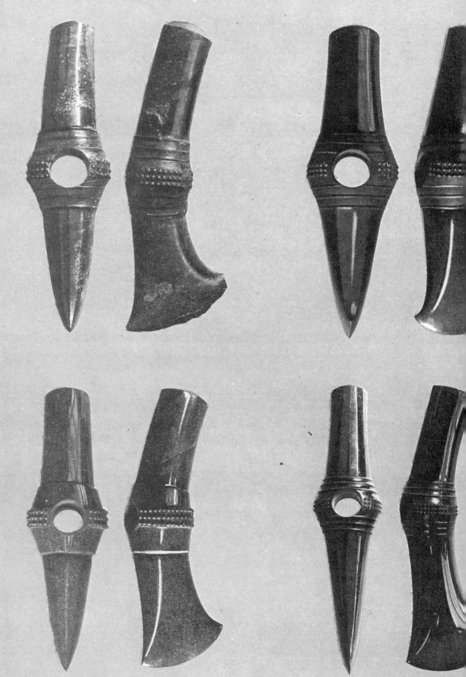

28

29

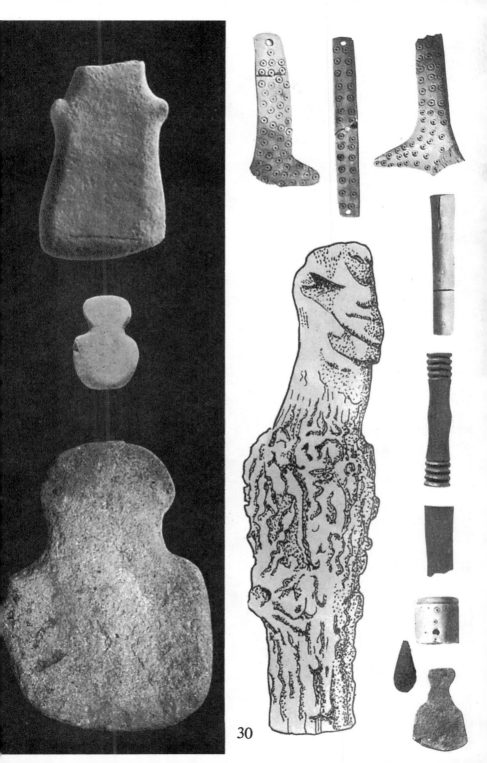

30

31

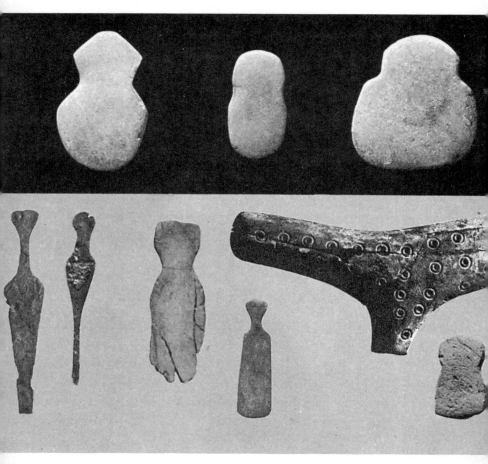

33

4

35

36

38

39

40

41

45

46

47

48

52

53

57

59

60

61

62

63

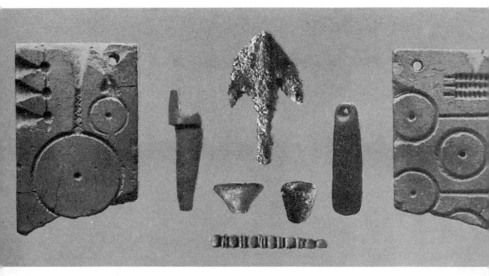

64

65

The Middle and Late Bronze Age: Troy VI

WITH TROY VI we find ourselves in the Middle Bronze Age, as reckoned in terms of the Aegean system of hronology. A survey of the ruins of the Sixth Settlement and f the miscellaneous objects and pottery recovered from them :veals at once striking differences and innovations as com⁄ ared with the preceding periods on the hill at Hissarlik. The hanges seem to me to be so unheralded, so widespread, and far⁄reaching that they can only be explained as indicating a reak with the past, and the arrival and establishment on the te of a new people endowed with a heritage of its own.

The spirit of change manifests itself in many fields of activity nd expression. It is obvious in the magnitude and splendour at characterise the transformation of the citadel once again to a powerful royal stronghold. The imposing fortifications at now rise display increased knowledge of military engineer⁄ g together with technical advances in masonry. The initial ppearance of distinctive vertical offsets, cut at almost regular tervals on the outer face of the wall, is a new phenomenon. he general scheme of laying out the settlement with its free⁄ anding houses, widely spaced on ascending ringed terraces, troduces a fresh concept of town⁄planning. The buildings emselves in their simple, straightforward design and their lid enduring structure testify to a new vigour and directness f purpose.

The miscellaneous objects from the sixth layer likewise troduce numerous items that have not been discovered in rlier deposits. Most of the evidence, it must be pointed out, mes from the Late Subperiod of Troy VI, the ruins of which ere examined in relatively large areas and which produced y far the greatest part of the material collected; but many of

Plate 38

Plate 51

the innovations must surely go back to the earliest phases o
the Sixth Settlement, whose strata were accessible to investi
gation only in much restricted areas at great depths, and yielde
only correspondingly scanty remains.

Although very little in the way of actual metals was recov
ered, real bronze was probably much more generally used than
previously; this conclusion is supported by the discovery o
three or four well-made, slender bronze knives, and there ar
also numerous whetstones of two new and more efficient types
Several pommels of stone, found in early as well as late con
texts of Troy VI, of shapes quite different from their predeces
sors of the Early Bronze Age, offer evidence that swords wer
not rare on the site. Ivory, too, becomes fairly well known in
Late VI, when terracotta pellets, loom weights of two new
shapes, and beads also seem to be made and used. Terracott
whorls continue to occur in the same profusion as heretofore
but an examination of the shapes represented reveals consider
able changes in the incidence of some types and the virtua
abandonment of incised decoration which was highly popula

Plates 56, 57

in Troy II to V inclusive.

A study of the pottery found in stratified deposits of th
Sixth Settlement bears out the evidence of the miscellaneou

Fig. 30

objects. The Cincinnati Expedition had originally planned t
prepare a comprehensive chart for the whole Bronze Age t
illustrate all the different distinguishable shapes of pots mad
and used in each of the successive periods. For Troy I to V
it proved to be a fairly homogeneous collection with a few new
types appearing from time to time but with many main line
of continuity running through. When Troy VI was reached
however, it became clear that a wholly new repertory of shape
was evolved to displace the old; and separate charts for the two
eras were consequently judged necessary. For the Sixth Settle
ment some 98 varieties of shape were differentiated and classi
fied. Among them 90 are new and only seven or eight seem t

ave any connection with the Trojan past. Those eight, how ver, are represented – mainly in Early VI – not by whole or early complete pots, but by scattered sherds too scanty for the econstruction of a single vessel. It is probable that there were few survivals from Troy V for a short time, but many of these ragments are evidently strays that somehow accidentally made heir way up from underlying strata. In any event there must ave been a virtually complete wholesale change of household rockery on the citadel at the beginning of Troy VI.

At the same time one further important novelty made its ppearance on the hill. That was the horse, whose bones were ot found by the Cincinnati Expedition in any of the earlier ayers. In the stratum representing the first phase of the Sixth ettlement horsebones came to light, and henceforth they ontinued to occur more or less frequently in all subsequent trata. The newcomers who at the start of the Middle Bronze \ge assumed domination over the site must have brought long the horse, an advantage that no doubt gave them uperiority over the Trojans of the Early Bronze Age.

In the central region of the citadel almost no remains of `roy VI were left to archaeologists for modern stratigraphic xcavation. For the whole top of the mound had been shaved ff in Hellenistic and Roman times in order to provide an open ourt around the Temple of Athena; what little, if anything, irvived was later for the most part dug away by Schliemann. ut along the outer periphery of the acropolis, on the east, uth, and southwest, undisturbed deposits still lay to a depth f 5 to 6 m. or more inside the line of the great fortification all. On the southern and eastern flanks of the hill this massive ccumulation, when tested by the Cincinnati Expedition, was und to be composed of eight successive strata, one above the ther, which were numbered in the sections from VIa to VIh. Vhether they correspond to actual differentiated phases or not, ey do in any event give us a real chronological sequence in

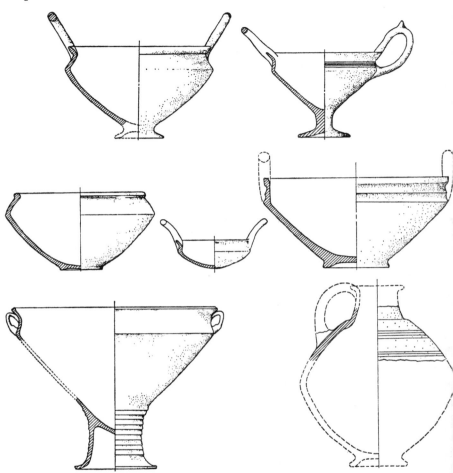

Fig. 30 Characteristic shapes of Grey Minyan Ware, Troy VI

which a course of gradual change and development is observ
able. It is clear that the settlement maintained its existence
without any signs of a cultural break through many centuries
passing from the Middle well down into the Late Bronze Age

In that long evolution it is possible to recognise three general stages which, following the usual system, we call Early, Middle, and Late VI.

In the monumental fortification walls, which are the glory of the Sixth Settlement, three successive projects in the construction of the fortress seem to be represented; and they may perhaps safely be correlated with the three stages just mentioned.

Plate 38

The great walls of Troy VI belong for the most part to the Late Subperiod of that settlement; but they are by no means of uniform style throughout. Some sections differ appreciably

Fig. 31

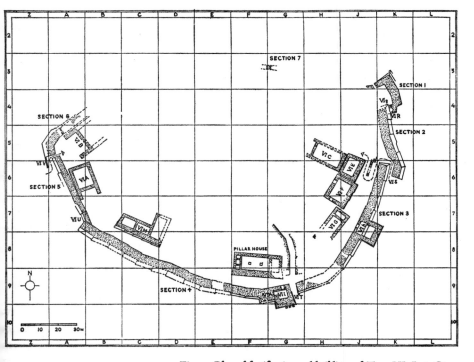

Fig. 31 Plan of fortification and buildings of Troy VI, Late Stage

from their neighbours both in materials and in technique. Dörpfeld, who had a keen eye for such architectural details, offered an ingenious and convincing explanation of the differences. He suggested that the imposing walls were built in the late years of the city to replace an earlier system of defence, and that the work was carried out gradually, one section at a time; thus the whole undertaking required for its completion a considerable span of years during which building methods and technical skill continued to improve. For some unknown reason one relatively short section of the older wall was never replaced, but was left standing just as it was. That is the southwestern wall, which we have called Section 5 on the plan. On the basis of the evidence available, the Cincinnati Expedition concluded that this piece of the wall had been built toward the end of the Middle Subperiod.

Directly behind it and almost parallel is another wall of the same general kind, but much less monumental. Dörpfeld, who discovered it, recognised it as still another fortification wall. Since it lay to a great extent beneath a large house (VI A) of the Sixth Settlement, much too important to be destroyed, and since it also stood so close behind its successor, Section 5, that it could not be adequately exposed for study, he was unable to ascertain full details of its structure, although he did observe the batter of its outer face and the presence of vertical offsets. As this wall was obviously older than Section 5, Dörpfeld attributed it to the Fifth Settlement, not knowing that the beginning of Troy VI goes far back into the Middle Bronze Age. The Cincinnati Expedition, which first found the deep deposits representing the Early Subperiod of the Sixth Settlement, judged that this wall must be assigned not to Troy V but to one of the early phases of Troy VI. Each of the three subperiods, Early, Middle, and Late VI, thus appears to have built its own system of fortification walls; and some distinctive features of construction link all three together.

Corroborative evidence has been observed on the south side of the circuit, where three successive gateways were built during *Figs. 31, 32* the period, each one in turn giving access from outside to the main thoroughfare that ascended to the higher quarters of the fortress. The oldest of the three, called Gate VI Z, was ascribed by the Cincinnati Expedition to the Early Subperiod, the next following, Gate VI Y, to Middle VI, while the third and last, Gate VI T, is a work of the Late Subperiod.

Too little of the first and second systems of fortification has survived and is visible for us to judge either of them as a whole. The third in chronological order is in any event by far the most ambitious and impressive. It is still preserved from the northeastern corner in a broad swing around the southern and western borders of the acropolis to the extreme northwestern angle, a total distance of some 350 m. The whole northern part of the circuit is missing, however, except for a small remnant in Square G 3; but this, though not more than 4 or 5 m. long, is sufficient to demonstrate – if a demonstration were needed – that the wall originally enclosed the entire citadel. Its demolition along the northern edge of the hill was for the most part carried out in Hellenistic and Roman times, although Schliemann's early campaigns may have taken their toll. With its five unevenly spaced gateways, the surviving part of the circuit divides itself naturally into six divisions or sections, which might be called the northeastern, eastern, southeastern, southern, southwestern, and northwestern walls, and which we have labelled on the plan as Sections 1 to 6.

We begin our description with the huge tower that forms the mighty northeastern bastion of the fortress. Still standing at Plate 39 its northern angle to a height of 26 courses, it is perhaps the finest piece of masonry in the whole circuit of the wall. Measuring about 18 m. in length from north to south, with an inside width of 8 m. or more, it is built of squared blocks of hard durable limestone, carefully laid and fitted together, though in

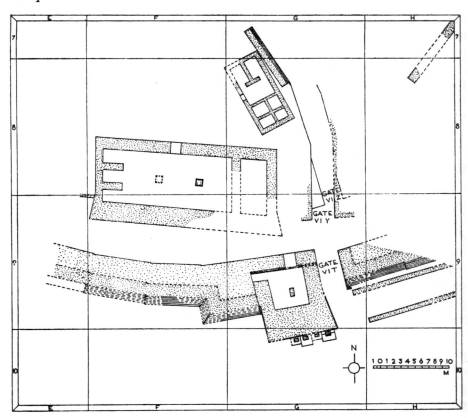

Fig. 32 Plan of South Gate, earlier gates, Pillar House and House 630

courses of somewhat irregular height, with particular attention to the alternation of joints from course to course. With its sharp acute angle projecting toward the north, and its characteristic profile – occasioned by an appreciable change in the degree of the batter of the outer face some 3 m. above the bottom – this tower is one of the most familiar published landmarks of Troy. Its handsome exterior stonework, as measured by Dörpfeld,

Plate 40

rose about 9 m. above the rock at its northern foot, and more than 1.50 m. above the floor inside the tower; but this under⁄ part supported a further high superstructure of crude brick, substantial remnants of which were observed and recorded by Dörpfeld. The lofty Northeast Tower was no doubt an ob⁄ servation post, dominating not only the acropolis but the whole Trojan plain that lay spread out below.

Inside the tower is a well, or cistern, approximately square, its open shaft measuring about 4.25 m. on a side; it was lined all around with a massive stone wall, 2 m. thick, that extended some 2 m. down below the floor to native rock. From this point the shaft, hewn in the rock itself, continued down to a further depth of 7 or 8 m. Too large to be a normal well, too deep for an ordinary cistern, it may have been intended to serve both purposes, as Dörpfeld shrewdly conjectured. Overhang⁄ ing walls prevented clearing of the bottom of the shaft. A stone stairway led up from the floor of the tower toward the west, providing access to the water supply for those coming down from the higher ground inside the citadel.

At its southern extremity the tower was extended in a pro⁄ jecting anta⁄like structure, which overlapped the northern end of the next section of the fortification wall, leaving a narrow passage between the two. This area was fitted out as a small gateway which had a door at its southern end and, at the northern, a flight of four stone steps that led down to the floor inside the tower. The door, which turned on a pivot, could swing back into a recess in the eastern side of the passage. This was evidently a postern gate that facilitated communication between the tower and the outside world.

The Northeast Tower was certainly added to the defensive works after the completion of Section 2, which extends on towards the south. Its main purpose was presumably to enclose the well⁄cistern within the fortification and thus to ensure a safe supply of water in emergencies.

The Eastern Wall, Section 2, some 41.50 m. long, runs from the Northeast Gate to the East Gate. At its northern end, as we have seen, it was overlapped by the east wall of the Northeast Tower, and at its southern end it overlaps in turn the next succeeding Section 3. Though not so elegant in its finish as the Northeast Tower, this second section is an admirable example of the technical skill and competence attained by the planners and builders when Troy VI had neared the zenith of its power. More than 4.50 m. thick and exceeding 4 m. in height, the wall was constructed of hard limestone blocks and slabs, efficiently shaped, solidly fitted together, and laid in more or less regular courses, large stones being freely used in the lower part, smaller material in the upper part of the wall. Four vertical offsets in the sloping face of the wall mark it off into five segments averaging a little over 8 m. in length and separated by slight angles. Much of the wall still survives, but it is not very accessible to view, for a massive Roman foundation runs directly across it and in front of it, hiding it largely from sight. Schliemann's Northeast Trench was driven straight through the wall, and very difficult digging it must have been to dislodge those tightly wedged blocks.

The East Gateway, separating Sections 2 and 3, takes the form of a passage about 2 m. wide and 5 m. long between the overlapping walls; it turns sharply inward around the northern end of Section 3. Scanty remains beyond the turn show that there was at one time an actual door that could be opened and closed; it was, as Dörpfeld noted, evidently an afterthought installed in the latest phase of Troy VI. The gateway was well planned for resistance to attack; the defenders could hurl their missiles from the top of the wall from both sides of the passage as well as from its inner end upon the attackers crowded into the narrow approach to the closed door around the corner.

The Third or Southeast Section of the wall, built in exactly the same style and no doubt at the same time as the Second, is

Plate 41

Plate 44

Plate 42

about 90 m. long, extending from the East Gate to the South
Gate. In this stretch nine vertical offsets on the outer face of the
wall divide it, as Dörpfeld phrased it, into ten straight sides of
a polygon, with somewhat unequal angles, but based on a
radius of approximately 100 m. Although the southern part of
this section was badly damaged by the construction directly
over it of a Roman Bouleuterion, or Council Chamber, as
well as by the digging of Schliemann's Southeast Trench, the
northern half of the unit is relatively well preserved and still
eloquently demonstrates the wealth and power of the rulers
under whom this formidable project was carried out.

The effect today would be even more striking if the stately
projecting tower – called by Dörpfeld VI h – near the middle
of Section 3, had survived in an equally good condition. Even
in its somewhat dilapidated state, however, it testifies to the
solid strength of the citadel in the Late Subperiod of Troy VI.
The tower was evidently an added feature, built in the final
phase of the Sixth Settlement as a further protection of the
East Gate.

Moving on to the southern terminus of Section 3 in Square
G 9, we come to the South Gate which was not formed by the
overlapping of walls: it was a simple opening or gap, 3.30 m.
wide, between the vertical ends of Sections 3 and 4. As
Dörpfeld recognised, this was the principal entrance to the
fortress, and a relatively broad street ascended from it toward
the upper terraces of the citadel. In its original state the gateway
was protected by a tower (VI k) about 7 m. wide, which stood
nearly 9 m. to the west of the gateway; it projected rather more
than 5 m. southward from the face of the wall, the latter having
been set back some 3.50 m. to the north of the line of Section 3.
This arrangement created a miniature court or recess in front of
the entrance, but garrison troops from the wall and the tower
could fire at aggressors from both sides and also from the front.
Later, probably in the final phase of Troy VI, a much grander

Plate 47

Plate 45

tower (VI i) was erected on the west side, directly beside th
entrance; it was approximately 10 m. wide and it projected
just over 10 m. southward from the wall. Jutting out 5.50 m
beyond the line of Section 3, it filled the earlier recess and
reduced the area through which assailants could approach
while giving the defenders still greater advantage. In its mate
rials and technique this tower is exactly like Tower VI h near
the East Gate.

The southern unit of the fortification wall, Section 4, pro
ceeds from the South Gate to the Southwest Gate, a total
distance of some 121 m. In this long stretch there are 13 vertica
offsets, with varying angles, dividing the wall into 14 straigh
segments which have an average length of nearly 9 m. Through
out its whole extent this section seems to be founded solidly on
native rock. It was built in a sophisticated style of neatly, no
to say elegantly, worked blocks of hard limestone of varying
sizes, fitted together with great care. As in other sections, large
blocks are regularly used in the lowest courses, smaller piece
in the upper. The masonry shows remarkable uniformity and
regularity in its coursing, and much attention was devoted to a
systematic alternation of jointing from one course to the next
After the wall had been built the vertical offsets received their
finishing touches, and the whole inclined face of the wall wa
smoothly dressed from top to bottom so that it offered a surface
very difficult to scale. A sturdy vertical breastwork no doub
rose high above the top of the sloping wall, with a platform
behind it.

Plate 43

The structure as a whole takes its place as a masterpiece o
military engineering of the Late Bronze Age. Some idea of it
grandeur can be gained – with the aid of a little imagination –
from a study of the segments nearest the South Gate, which
were to a considerable degree protected from injury by the grea
tower built in front of them; and one's admiration is likewise
stirred by some of the less well-preserved remains of the segment

lying farther to the west. But the greater part of the wall has suffered much damage inflicted especially on its outer face by the construction in late classical and in Roman Imperial times of a small theatre or odeum and many other public buildings and sanctuaries that were erected one after another abutting against the face of the wall or embedded in its core.

The South Wall terminated toward the west in Square A 7 in a vertical end, nearly 5 m. thick in its upper part. This was evidently designed to serve as one side of a Southwest Gateway, called by Dörpfeld VI U. At this point there had undoubtedly been a gate and a sharp angle in the older circuit, which was now, in the Late Subperiod, in process of being replaced on a more ambitious scale. For some reason, unknown to us and not obvious, that project was apparently not carried to comple-tion. The old gateway was no longer left open for traffic, but was closed by a solid wall of stones; and the next unit of the fortification, Section 5, the Southwest Wall, was allowed to stand without replacement. As already noted, this unit must surely be the last surviving element of the earlier circuit belong-ing to the Middle Subperiod of Troy VI. It is not properly incorporated into the new system, and its relation to Section 4 on the east and Section 6 toward the northwest is awkward, to say the least. The archaic wall has only half the thickness of the new, and is far less strong. It is built of much smaller stones, and its foundations were not carried down to rock. But it has a considerable batter on its outer face and it has the vertical offsets that seem to be distinctive in all phases of Troy VI.

When the project of reconstruction was abandoned the old wall was patched and repaired in several places, especially alongside Gate VI U. The patching was done by masons who were familiar with the new style of building favouring the use of large stones.

At the northwest end of the archaic wall in Square A 5 we come to another gateway (VI V). This one, too, was merely

Plate 46

a gap between two units of the wall, Sections 5 and 6, th
latter set forward toward the west some 5 m. beyond the lin
of the former. The opening between the two was only abou
2.50 m. wide, rather narrow for a gateway of any importance
Approach to the entrance from outside the citadel was evidentl
from the southeast by a roadway that ascended alongsid
Section 5 and then turned sharply eastward through the open
ing. Attackers would have their right sides exposed to missile
of defenders stationed on the wall above and would also hav
to face frontal fire from the top of the Northwest Wall.

The latter, Section 6, which was first uncovered in 1935 an
1937, and which had been built in the same grandiose style a
the South Wall, could be traced some 35 m. toward the nortl
and the northeast. Only the lower courses of the foundation
are preserved, the upper part having apparently served as a
quarry in Hellenistic and Roman times; but even in thei
wreckage they display an unmistakable magnificence. It i
clear that this is a work of the same period as the South Wal
probably of Phase VI g. Beyond the last surviving stones tha
can be identified as still in place, and for a distance of mor
than 100 m. along the northern edge of the hill, no remains o
the wall now exist. But two short segments, still recognisabl
in Squares F–G 3, one of Early VI, the other of the Lat
Subperiod, are certainly remnants of the North Wall; and it i
probable that the later of the two represents a seventh section
perhaps contemporary with the East and South Towers.

The fortifications of Troy VI shed abundant light on th
architectural achievements of the late Sixth Settlement. But a
kindly fortune has also preserved for us remains of several o
the notable houses that once stood within the citadel. Th
royal palace, which presumably occupied the summit of th
hill, vanished from sight in ancient times, giving way to th
temple of Athena and its court; and the houses on the nex
lower terrace suffered a like fate. On the lowest terrace, how

Plate 48

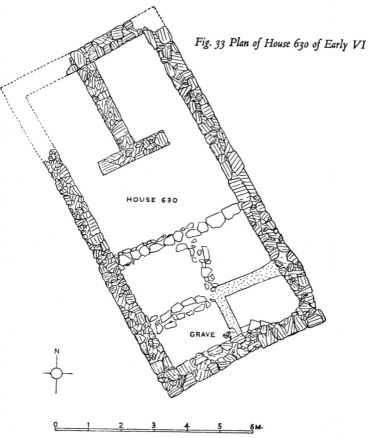

Fig. 33 Plan of House 630 of Early VI

HOUSE 630

GRAVE

N

0 1 2 3 4 5 6M.

ever, just above and roughly parallel to the fortress walls, Dörpfeld uncovered remains of eight or nine buildings, to which one more was added in the years 1932 to 1937. Considerable parts of one house and scanty remnants of two or three others had also been recognised in 1893–94 on the second terrace from the bottom, but nothing standing on higher levels has survived. Before considering these large resi⸗

dences which begin in Middle VI and belong mainly to La
VI we should glance briefly at a much smaller house of th
Early Subperiod.

This is House 630, oriented roughly from north to south
nearly all of which lies in Square G 8. It seems to have bee
built in Phase VIa, and its walls were made with a relativel

Fig. 33 high stone socle supporting a superstructure of crude brick
It is a free-standing, single house, quite different from th
multiple dwellings seen in Troy V. Originally it may have ha
its entrance at the south end, possibly with a portico that le
into a principal room from which doorways opened into tw
chambers behind. Later, the southern part was divided b
narrow partitions of crude brick into four small cubicles, an
a new doorway may have been made in the middle of the lon
western side. In the straightforwardness of its plan and in th
neatness of its walls, built of smallish slabs of limestone lai
in fairly regular courses, this house surely represents an earl
stage in the building technique that reached its full develop
ment in the Late Subperiod.

Remains of at least 17 houses of that age have been exposed
almost all found and numbered by Dörpfeld in 1893–94
Nine of them – Houses VI D, VI H, VI J, VI K, VI L
VI N, VI O, VI P, and VI Q – are too incomplete to allov
much – if anything – to be said regarding their original plan
The others show not a little variety in their design. Five wei

Fig. 31 relatively long in proportion to their width, resembling at firs
glance the type often called *megaron*. These are the building
designated by Dörpfeld as VI A, VI B, VI C, and VI G
together with one uncovered by the Cincinnati Expedition an
named the Pillar House.

House VI A, lying mainly in Squares A–B 6, was dis
covered and partly cleared by Schliemann and Dörpfeld i
1890 and was fully exposed by the latter in 1893. It was hei
that Mycenaean pottery was first found in any quantity on th

site. Little more than the foundations of the house are preserved, and even they are incomplete. They are well built of large stones in their lower part, and the superstructure seems to have been made of smaller rectangular blocks. The house, 19.18 m. long and 12.30 m. wide, comprised a portico, 4.25 m. deep, and a single large room, 11.55 m. long and 9.10 m. wide. The floor has not survived, and no evidence of column bases was observed. But the span of 9.10 m. from side to side is rather formidable, and it is likely that wooden pillars were used to help support the roof. The building, facing southeastward, bears a strong resemblance to the *megaron*-like palace II A of the Second Settlement.

Directly to the north of House VI A Dörpfeld recognised remains of a second similar but larger structure, which he called VI B. Only the portico, which faces southwestward, and scanty parts of the main chamber now survive, but the proportions – as compared with House VI A – suggest that the building originally measured roughly 16 by 25 m. Here too the floor is missing and there are no remains of column bases, but it is surely safe to assume that interior supports of some kind were employed.

Not far from the eastern end of the acropolis, in Squares H–J 5–6, are the ruins of House VI C, which stood on the lowest but one of the concentric ascending terraces. Although the middle part of the building was cut away in the digging of Schliemann's Northeast Trench, the walls that were then removed were first measured and recorded; and the plan of the house as a whole was thus preserved by Dörpfeld. This too looks like a *megaron*, facing toward the northwest. Its exterior dimensions are 10.90 by 20.07 m., and it seems to have comprised a single great room, 8.40 m. wide and 15.50 m. long, with a shallow portico, 2.05 m. deep, apparently opening toward the northwest. A shaped column base of stone still survives in the northwestern part of the large chamber, and it

Fig. 34

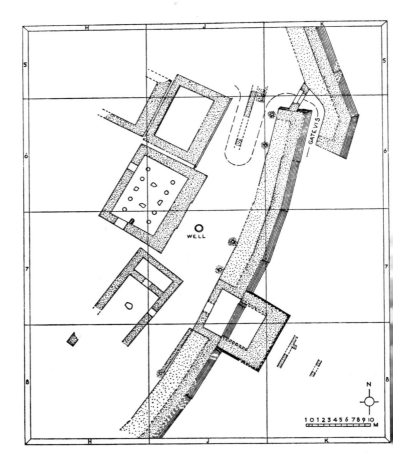

Fig. 34 Plan of eastern side of citadel, Troy VI: Houses VI C, VI E, VI F and VI G, and East Gate. (cf. Fig. 31, p. 115)

indicates that there was probably a row of three such bases fo. wooden pillars spaced along the longitudinal axis, and sup. porting the ceiling and roof. Dörpfeld was inclined to believe that this was a true *megaron*, but he called attention to the fac

hat there is no decisive evidence of a doorway between the hall
nd the vestibule: the dividing wall is still so high here that two
teps would be needed to enable one to cross it from the floor
f the hall to the level of the vestibule. Traces of a narrow
pening were noted at the south end of the eastern wall, but
ne workmanship is so careless that it may represent a later
lteration. The position of the principal entrance therefore
emains unknown.

One of the most remarkable peculiarities of the building is
nat the two lateral walls are not parallel to each other, but
onverge slightly in their course toward the northwest, the
whole plan being thus slightly trapezoidal. The same oddity
ppears in the neighbouring houses, VI E and VI F, as well
s in other houses and in Towers VI h and VI i. All were laid
ut deliberately in this way along converging lines, radiating
om the centre of the citadel. It is obvious that some powerful
uthority controlled the planning of the houses in the acropolis.
Dörpfeld, who first observed this convergence of the lines of
ne buildings, suggested that the purpose was to enable all the
treets and passages that climbed toward the upper quarters of
ne fortress to maintain their normal width all the way up
nstead of being compressed and narrowed by right-angled
onstruction on either side.

House VI G, in Squares H–J 7–8, is of a somewhat com-
arable type. It seems to have been approximately 20.90 m.
ong and 9.40 m. wide, running roughly from north to south.
t had the misfortune to lie in the path of Schliemann's broad
outheast Trench, which cut away almost the entire southerly
nird of the building. How the latter terminated toward the
outh is therefore not certainly ascertainable, though Dörpfeld
vas tempted to believe that a portico led in from that direction,
iving access to a long main hall, behind which lies a small
ear chamber. In 1936 the original earthen floor of the house
vas reached, and on it was found a large stone base obviously

Fig. 34

Plate 49

intended to support a wooden column. Not far away, now lying at the bottom of Schliemann's trench that cut through the house, is a second block of the same general size and character; and it may fairly be deduced that the long hall originally had at least two columns standing along its major axis. In its general arrangement it thus follows the same pattern as that we have seen in House VI C. Like the latter, however it offers several puzzling problems in detail.

In the southeastern wall of House VI G, approximately 7 m. from the northeast corner, clear traces of a doorway are still preserved: the horizontal cavity, in which a large wooden threshold was once fitted, and two smaller cavities beneath it for wooden blocks to which the sill had once been nailed, along with scanty remains of the stone door jambs on each side. The exact width of the opening is not certain, but it probably exceeded 1.20 m. A noticeable feature of what is left of the door jambs on either side is the high polish caused by persons rubbing against them when going in and out; and this proves that we are dealing with a doorway rather than a window. But it is a remarkably awkward entrance to a house. For the ground level outside lay 0.48 m. below the top of the threshold; and the floor inside was still lower by 0.40 m. This meant that at least two steps were needed to reach the threshold from outside, while four were necessary for the descent to the floor inside. It is likely that a wooden platform, or landing, had to be built inside the room and possibly another one outside. This most singular installation of a stairway must definitely be assigned to the latest phase of Troy VI, for it clearly antedated a reconstruction and a reoccupation of the building that can be attributed to Period VIIa. The many storage jars or *pithoi* found in House VI G, some of which were discovered by Dörpfeld and ascribed by him to Troy VI, were judged by the Cincinnati Expedition to have been introduced in the following period, Troy VIIa.

In the excavations conducted from 1932 to 1938 still another building of comparable type was brought to light. That
is the Pillar House, as it has been called, standing in Squares
F–G 8–9. It is one of the largest structures yet found at Troy,
being more than 26 m. long and exceeding 12 m. in width.
Its foundation walls, running approximately from east to west,
are correspondingly massive, especially the one on the south,
2.92 m. thick, which serves also as a retaining wall; this is
certainly a re-used surviving part of an earlier construction,
probably a fortification wall of Middle or Early VI. Like
Houses VI C, VI E, and VI F, this huge building has a
trapezoidal plan, its southern side being considerably longer
than the northern, with the two ends laid along converging
lines.

The Pillar House was designed with a relatively small room,
about 3.80 m. wide, extending across its eastern end, a great
hall, about 15.50 m. long and 8 m. wide, occupying the
middle section, and three little compartments, or cubicles, side
by side across the western end. The roof of the building,
probably flat, was supported by the outside walls and cross-
walls aided by two sturdy pillars set along the axis of the great
hall. One of these, built of carefully worked, squared blocks
of limestone, laid in the fashion of headers and stretchers, still
stands to a height of 1.70 m. above the floor. The other pillar,
which was destroyed by later intrusions, is represented only by
its substantial foundations; it was probably of the same structure and shape as its mate. The surviving pillar is approximately
square in section, measuring at the floor level about 1.07 m.
on a side; it tapers appreciably but somewhat unevenly, as it
rises, and at the top of the third course its dimensions have been
reduced to 0.80 by 0.74 m.

Small, neatly cut, square holes, about 0.04 m. on a side and
0.075 m. deep, were observed in the upper surface of some
exposed blocks. They are cuttings for dowels that fastened

Plate 50

Fig. 32

stones of a superposed course to those of the course below – a remarkable anticipation of one of the technical refinements in classical Greek architecture. In one instance, when the cracked corner of a block had to be cleaned and restored to its place, corresponding dowel-holes were found still undisturbed, one in the top of the lower stone, the other directly above it in the bottom of the upper block. Only fine dust remained in the hole, giving no clue as to the material of which the dowels themselves were made. There was in any event no trace of metal, and it may be conjectured that suitably shaped pieces of wood or some other perishable substance were used.

The Pillar House, like Houses VI A, VI B, VI C, and VI G, looks at first glance as if it might fairly be called a *megaron*; but closer examination reveals no evidence that there was ever a doorway in the eastern end. Instead, approximately at the middle of the long hall, a flight of three stone steps led up against the north wall, and there can be no doubt that there was a doorway here. Indeed, scratches on the top step show that double doors set on pivots swung inward into the room. The presence of a side entrance, at all events, makes it clear that the Pillar House cannot be regarded as a normal *megaron*.

The building was apparently occupied, with various altera-tions, through all the phases of the Late Subperiod of Troy VI. One of its earliest elements is a large rectangular area, paved with stones, in the southwestern corner of the main hall; it supported a structure perhaps framed and partitioned by thin walls of crude brick. In the northwestern corner of the room was a hearth on a stone platform in the centre of which a coarse pot had been set. Several small areas of the latest floor baked hard by fire evidently mark the site of casual hearths. A large space in the northwestern part of the hall was at some time walled off, evidently as a place where cooking could be done. Within it a large circular domed oven was also installed. The three small cubicles at the western end belong to the

Plate 50

original plan; later they were shut off from the main hall by stone walls of undetermined height; and their floors were paved with flattish stones. No evidence was forthcoming to disclose the original purpose of these little compartments.

The abundant miscellaneous objects and pottery recovered in the Pillar House provide valuable evidence for the chronology of the successive floors and strata representing Phases VIf, VIg, and VIh; but they do not firmly establish the original purpose for which this monumental building was designed. The many terracotta pellets found there, together with the fact that the structure was near to the principal gateway, might suggest that it was a military establishment connected with the defence of the citadel. On the other hand, innumerable spindle whorls and many loom weights, also of terracotta, might lead one to think of a spinnery or a workshop where textiles were woven. But on the evidence of numerous beads of paste and terracotta and much ordinary household pottery, one may conclude that in Phase VIh at least, it was probably occupied as a dwelling-house. It is one of the most interesting buildings in the Sixth Settlement.

House VI E, standing on a terrace in Squares J 5–6, though much smaller than its neighbours, can boast a retaining wall built in as fine a style of masonry as any that has survived from Troy VI. This building has a trapezoidal plan with converging north and south sides in the fashion favoured at Troy. Approximately 10.10 m. wide, it has a length from north to south varying from 13.35 to 12.80 m. Disturbances at the end of the period and in later times destroyed almost all the superstructure of the house and left no part of the original floor in place. Consequently we can only guess at the internal arrangement of the single large room which seems to occupy the whole area. It is likely that there was a doorway centred in the northern wall, and, although no stone column bases have been found, there may have been one or two wooden posts to help support

Plate 51

Plate 52

133

the roof. The latter was presumably flattish, with a tilt to shed water, and made of horizontal wooden timbers laid close together and holding up a thick layer of earth and clay, perhaps topped with sand or gravel.

Directly to the south of House VI E and separated from it by a space of less than 1 m., is a much larger structure also of *Plate 53, Fig. 35* trapezoidal design. This is House VI F, which was discovered and partly excavated by Dörpfeld in 1893-94, and which was further investigated and cleared to its floor some 40 years later by the Cincinnati Expedition. The walls, all massively built, almost in cyclopean style, are of different thicknesses on all four sides. Each has an inner and outer face made of large roughly shaped blocks, laid in somewhat irregular courses with small stones and chips filling interstices and cracks, while the central core is composed of smaller stones less regularly fitted together. In the south, west, and north walls may be seen a broad horizontal cavity, or slot, in which a great wooden beam was once fitted, to serve as a reinforcement or framework. Beams of this kind were inserted into both the inner and outer faces of the three walls mentioned. Though not so regular, this method of building walls is comparable to that exemplified in Mycenaean architecture, as seen, for example, in the palaces at Mycenae and Pylos. There it has sometimes been explained as an anti-seismic device to keep the stones in the wall from shifting; but it may also or alternatively be an inherited tradition from early construction in crude brick.

The eastern foundation of House VI F is the most monumental, being 2.66 m. thick; it spreads outward in two *Plate 54* or three irregular steps toward the bottom, where it rests on earth, 3.80 m. below the floor of the house. Two relatively deep vertical offsets divide the outer face of the wall into three sections. The superstructure along this eastern side is not preserved, and what its thickness was above the floor level is not known.

Fig. 35 Plan of House VI F, Middle and Late VI

The floor of the house was made of earth packed hard and covered with a thin coating of reddish clay; it was somewhat uneven and also sloped downward from west to east, its level beside the east wall being 0.45 m. deeper than that alongside the west wall. Two rows of shaped stone column bases, five in each row, some rising considerably, others only slightly above the floor, divide the interior of the building into a nave and two lateral aisles in the fashion of a basilica; and two further bases of irregular shape stand in the longitudinal axis of the nave, sunk deep below the floor. Though the two sets of column bases might conceivably have served different purposes in one and the same installation, it is not unlikely that they represent two periods. There is, moreover, some evidence to suggest that the house had two stories.

Dörpfeld noted that two doorways gave access into House VI F, one near the northern end of the western side, the other not far from the western end of the south wall. This latter opening was closed and filled with a blocking wall of stones before the Sixth Settlement was destroyed. The other doorway leads in from the west, where the ground level immediately outside the building was at least 2 m. higher than the floor inside the house. At the south end of the three-aisled hall, just to the right as one entered the door, a large stone block still remains in its original place; it is a step, evidently the lowest in a stairway, the rest of which was probably built of wooden timbers, that ascended to an upper floor or the roof. It was presumably installed after the south door was blocked with its stone filling and could no longer be used as an entrance. The lower apartment was thus converted into a basement accessible only by the interior staircase from the upper storey. The western doorway must then have served as the entrance to the house.

Any attempt to reconstruct the upper part of the building and its roof encounters numerous uncertainties and problems. The thickness of the walls and the multiple interior columns certainly imply that there was a substantial upper storey. The roof itself was probably flat; there are various possibilities regarding its exact arrangement, and even a clerestory is not excluded. In the absence of evidence, however, all conclusions are conjectural.

It is obvious in any event that House VI F was long occupied and no doubt saw many a change from time to time. In
a late, but not the final, phase of Troy VI the southwest corner
of the lower floor seems to have been transformed into a
kitchen. A stone-paved hearth in the form of a quarter-circle
was built in the angle between the south and west walls,
bordered by rough stone orthostates. The lower half of a large
jar was sunk deep into the pavement, perhaps a place where
the fire could be preserved for long intervals in smouldering
coals. The whole corner was found filled with ashes and debris
along with broken pottery.

House VI F was first built in Phase VIe, toward the end
of the Middle Subperiod of Troy VI, and it evidently continued to be inhabited through the late phases VIf and VIg;
in Phase VIh the basement was partly filled with earth and
rubbish, and if used at all, was no more than a place for storage.
From the original – or earliest – deposit on the floor came a
considerable collection of imported Mycenaean pottery, comprising more than 20 pots decorated in a late stage of the
Palace Style, probably overlapping Mycenaean II and
Mycenaean III A, to use the system of classification introduced
by Furumark.

A plan wholly different from all the foregoing is that offered
by House VI M, which was discovered and exposed by
Dörpfeld in 1893–94. It lies in the southwestern part of the
acropolis, mainly in Squares C 7–8. Here we have an L-
shaped building, the long side oriented roughly from east to
west, the short arm extending northward from the eastern end.
The house stands on a lofty terrace, more than 4 m. high,
almost but not exactly parallel to the fortification wall, at a
distance of some 6 to 7 m. from the latter. The broad space
between was open in the time of Troy VI and was probably
used as a street. The terrace is supported by a magnificent
retaining wall, nearly 27 m. long, which once had a smoothly

Plates 46, 55

finished sloping outer face that is marked off by four vertical offsets into five segments. It is one of the most impressive surviving monuments of Troy VI.

The eastern wing of House VI M seems to have been given over to a single room or hall, more than 5 m. wide and 13 m. long. Its outer wall, toward the east, has been almost wholly destroyed. Still standing in their places along the western side of the large hall, were found six storage jars; and the northern quarter, marked off by a crumbling wall, may have been a kitchen where the household cooking was done. Several small pots, some millstones, and about 50 loom weights were recovered here, probably a deposit of Troy VIIa, since this house was reoccupied in that period. In the angle between the two wings of the L there was an open court from which one could no doubt enter the two chambers or storerooms that constituted the southern wing. On the opposite side of the court, toward the north, a flight of six stone steps is still preserved; the stairway to which they belonged evidently led up to the next higher terrace of the citadel.

The great houses of Troy VI which have been described at some length are worthy of consideration, for they certainly are distinctive, and even in their dilapidated state they convey some idea of the nature and character of their builders. These were obviously men of quality and substance, vigorous, creative, ready to act with strength and determination; they raised up this mightiest of all the strongholds that successively occupied the site; and they laid out the town inside it in a systematic and orderly manner. They did not neglect to pay careful attention to detail, but at the same time they possessed the vision and capacity to carry out a project of enduring grandeur.

Regarding the religious life of the Sixth Settlement little is known. Close alongside and parallel to the southern front of Tower VI i, stands a row of rectangular monolithic pillars or menhirs. Two of them were discovered in 1894 by Dörpfeld

Plate 45

who, no doubt rightly, interpreted them as evidence that a cult of some kind was associated with this area. Two more stones of the same character were exposed in the excavations of 1932–38. All four were truncated, and one was further dam‑ aged, since they chanced to stand in the way of construction in Roman times; just how high they originally rose can therefore not be determined, but the fact that they were set firmly in substantial foundations of large blocks indicates that they were tall. The four pillars do not take up all the space outside the tower; toward the west, where buildings of Troy IX were founded deep in the underlying deposit, there is ample room for two more stones, and it is probably safe to assume that there were once six all told.

They may be compared with the menhirs that have been found in Cyprus and Anatolia, and at a greater remove per‑ haps with the more elegant pillars and columns known in Minoan places of worship. It is possible that there was an actual shrine inside Tower VI i, for at its centre stands a raised base surrounded by a circular area paved with flat stones. On the top of the base are marks of weathering which indicate that it supported two columns standing close together. Since they apparently serve no structural purpose in this position, they may perhaps with greater plausibility be regarded as cult furniture. A long narrow building across the street, to the east of Tower VI i, was found to contain little or no normal house‑ hold pottery but many animal bones, and numerous patches of burning were noted on several successive floors where fires had often been lighted. Perhaps this too was a sanctuary where burnt sacrifices were frequently offered, possibly in connection with ceremonial arrivals or departures. At the Western Gate, VI V, a monolith similar to those outside Gate VI T stood in a comparable position. These architectural remains offer the only tangible evidence yet recognised bearing on religion in the Sixth Settlement.

Plate 51

Miscellaneous objects recovered from strata of Troy VI are relatively numerous; but, as noted by the excavators of 1893–9 and confirmed by those of 1932–38, very few of them possess artistic qualities at all commensurate with the magnificence of the fortification walls and the houses in the citadel. One possible and reasonable explanation of this discrepancy is the suggestion that nearly all the valuables were salvaged from the ruins of the settlement, either by the original owners or by successors who reoccupied and rebuilt most of the houses. In any event the chief importance of the many items collected – even if of little artistic worth – lies, as we have already seen, in that they provide supporting evidence of a cultural break between Troy V of the Early Bronze Age and Troy VI.

A part from its similar testimony regarding the break between the Fifth and the Sixth Settlements, the pottery of Troy VI offers much interest in itself. Here we have from the very beginning, Phase VIa, Grey Minyan Ware in a wide variety of characteristic shapes. At the outset it is virtually identical with the Minyan Ware found on Middle Helladic sites of the Greek mainland both in its technique and in the distinctive, largely angular shapes which it regularly assumes. This is not merely a grey ware such as presents itself in the Early Bronze Age at Troy, as well as in many widely dispersed areas, far and near: it is a recognisable special kind of grey fabric, inseparable from its own exclusive repertory of shapes that marks it off from other kinds. Handles in the form of animal heads are particularly characteristic of this period. At Troy we are not dealing merely with a few casual fragments of imported pots; the material comes from vessels that were turned out locally in abundance through a long period of time. For the Early Sub-period at least 21 shapes and varieties of shapes are represented; for Middle VI there are 26; and from deposits of Late VI, which were examined over a large area, the number has grown to 49 or more.

Plate 57

Fig. 30, Plate 56

There have been various theories about Minyan Ware. It was once thought to be a product manufactured from a special kind of clay at a centre from which it was widely distributed. Now it is known that almost any kind of clay will do. It was the method of firing the pots under reducing conditions that produced so generally the even grey colour. During the long era of its use from the beginning to the end of Troy VI Minyan Ware held tenaciously to its distinctive character, though it was by no means immune to change and development. This is particularly shown by the increase in the numbers and varieties of shapes that appear toward the close of the period, when pots of pure Mycenaean types, like the stirrup-vase, and the tall three-handled jar, were made in the technique of Minyan Ware. A similar, but not exactly the same, evolution, crossing Minoan-Mycenaean with Minyan, took place on the Helladic mainland.

Plate 56

At Troy, in Phase VIb and later, some fragments of Matt-painted pottery make their appearance alongside the Grey Minyan; few at first, but more numerous in the Middle Sub-period, they are probably not of local manufacture, but come presumably from fairly large vessels brought to the Troad from the west. The nearest parallels are to be found in central Greece and the Peloponnesos. In subsequent phases, beginning with VId, sherds of imported Mycenaean pots appear in increasing numbers. A few pieces of LH I, or Mycenaean I, have been found in deposits assignable to Phase VId; and from the stratum of VIe there are some examples in the style of Mycenaean II. In the Late Subperiod, strata of Phases VIf and VIg have yielded fragments of imported pots of Mycenaean II and III A; and at the end of the final Phase VIh, during which a good deal of Mycenaean pottery was imported, we find a preponderance of Mycenaean III A with an admixture of Mycenaean III B. This orderly sequence of the well-known Matt-painted and Mycenaean ceramic styles, coming from the

successive strata of Troy VI, offers us an invaluable chron,
ological framework on which to base our general dating of the
Sixth Settlement. It seems to have endured through a span of
half a millennium from about 1800 to 1300 BC with some
leeway at the beginning and the end.

Exploratory excavations along the edge of the plateau of
Ilion, some 550 m. south of the acropolis, in 1934 exposed a
small cemetery, which clearly belonged to the very end of Troy
VI. It was a burial ground of cinerary urns containing the
burned bones and ashes of adults and children as well as some
scanty remnants of objects that had been burned and buried
with them. Two jars of this kind had already been found in the
same region by Dörpfeld in 1893; but no wider investigation
was then undertaken. The Cincinnati Expedition, attracted to
the place by the numerous potsherds of Troy VI that lay strewn
on the ground, opened a considerable area and exposed to view
19 further urns, in various states of preservation, still standing
more or less undisturbed in their original positions. Their
survival was almost miraculous, not only because they were
covered with relatively little earth, but because a fortification
wall of Hellenistic times was built directly across the cemetery,
military trenches in 1915 were dug through it, and quarrying
in recent times also caused much damage. Fragments of human
bones and of many shattered urns lay scattered throughout the
neighbourhood. From a study of this material it was possible
to estimate that the burial ground had once held at least 200
jars, and probably a great many more.

These vessels and their contents cannot lay claim to any
notable intrinsic value. The pots, large and small, and the
sherds are distinctive and representative of Phase VIh. Among
the objects that had been deposited in the urns are three small
Mycenaean vases and 95 fragments of others, all probably
imported. The bulk of this collection may be assigned to
Furumark's category Mycenaean III A, but there are likewise

Plate 58

some pieces that must be put in III B. This tallies with the con/
clusions drawn from a study of the material found on the acro/
polis in the stratum of Phase VIh.

The importance of this discovery is twofold: it is the first and
only cemetery of pre/classical Troy that has yet become known,
and it shows that cremation was practised here in the final stage
of the Sixth Settlement. From the remnants of burned bones
recovered both in and outside the urns, Dr Angel was able to
determine that some 29 individuals were represented: 13 infants,
ranging from new/born to a few months old, seven women,
six men, and three of uncertain identification. It thus seems to
be an ordinary normal burial ground.

The custom of burning the dead was already familiar to the
Hittites at Boghaz/köy at about this same time, namely, near
the end of the fourteenth century B C or a little earlier. This is
known from the text of an inscribed tablet and from actual
remains that have been found. Was it a traditional custom at
Troy in the older phases of the Sixth Settlement, and even still
farther back in the Early Bronze Age? There is no evidence
and we do not know. A theory that cremation had been
adopted in earlier times on the site might provide a reasonable
explanation of the puzzling absence of cemeteries for all the
periods from Troy I to the latter part of VI. That, if verified,
would be a consolation to those who have sought long and
widely, but in vain, for tombs in the vicinity.

Troy VI came to its end in a tremendous catastrophe which
has left abundant testimony in many places along an area of
120 m. or more that follows the edge of the site from the East
Gate in Squares J–K 6 to an area in Squares F 8–9, well to the
west of the South Gate. Here the final stratum, VI h, was still
adequately preserved; elsewhere later disturbances have pene/
trated much too deeply.

The upper part of the fortification wall toppled over, some
of it outwards, but more inwards – perhaps because the found/

Plate 59

ations on this side were stepped back under the wall. The superstructures of the large houses that stood inside the fortress on the lower ring of terracing were also hurled down — mainly outwards because of the slope. In Square J 6 the wreckage was found to lie in a compact mass as if a substantial section of the wall must have fallen all together as a unit. The debris of House VI E on the western side of the peripheral roadway likewise collapsed in a mass. The magnitude of the sections that fell in this place and farther south surely points to a force beyond the power of human hands in an age before the invention of explosives and modern machinery of destruction. The Cincinnati Expedition was convinced that the disaster was the work of a violent earthquake that laid the whole citadel in ruins. Some pieces of carbonised wood came to light in various places and a few small deposits of ashes were noted; but there was no sign of a general conflagration, nor even of the destruction of a single house by fire. Burning and killing, which were of course the normal accompaniment of the capture and the sacking of a city in ancient times, seem to be lacking here. A further piece of evidence also carries much weight: in the succeeding period, Troy VIIa, we see that the fortification walls were immediately repaired and supplemented; some of the old houses were also reconstructed and reoccupied and many new ones built, filling almost all the available space inside the stronghold. The culture of Troy VI continues to prevail with no perceptible change, no sign of interruption or break, and Settlement VIIa embarks on its career with no trace of innovations from other regions, nothing to suggest a decline in, or an impoverishment of, the population. Relations with the western Mycenaean world are still maintained for a full generation or more. Dörpfeld and his staff in their report on the excavations of 1893–94 assert that Troy VII[1] (our VIIa) represents the same civilisation as that of the Sixth City, as a consequence of which they were unable to differentiate either the miscellaneous objects or the pottery of the one from those of the other. Dörpfeld in 1935 suggested that it might be well henceforth to substitute for Troy VIIa the designation Troy VIi. That would certainly correspond with the observed facts; but we have kept the established terminology in order to avoid confusing those who have long been familiar with it.

What people were these who established themselves on the hill of Troy and held it during the life of the Sixth Settlement, and who after the earthquake still continued to occupy it through Period VIIa? And whence did they come? These are questions which, in the absence of decisive evidence, cannot be answered with certainty. But surely we must recognise here a new element at Troy, different in origins and traditions from the occupants of the Early Bronze Age, an element forming part of a much larger movement which made itself felt through all the Eastern Mediterranean regions, extending through Syria and even to Egypt in those troubled times of change that accompanied the turn from the Early to the Middle Bronze Age. The mainland of Greece, too, was overrun in this same period, and it is in that direction that we must look, I believe, when seeking further light on the connections of the Trojans of the Sixth Settlement. The two invading groups, one on the east, one on the west side of the Aegean, make their appearance at the same time. They use the same technique in making pottery and they produce the same distinctive shapes of vessels in Grey Minyan Ware. To each region they bring with them a great innovation, the horse as their beast of burden. Through the whole ensuing period they keep up relations with one another. Must we not, therefore, conclude that these two groups were kinsmen, branches of one and the same stock? Many scholars now hold that the invaders who introduced Middle Helladic culture into Greece were actually the first Hellenic peoples to set foot in the peninsula. If that view is correct – and it seems to me to rest on well-founded arguments – we shall have to accept the further conclusion that the founders of Troy VI were also Greeks – the earliest of their race to gain a foothold in Asia Minor.

Regarding their origin and the earlier home from which they must have set out, no convincing theory has yet been put forward. Whether they came wandering down from the north to the Aegean, or arrived in ships by way of the Black Sea and the Straits from southern Russia, or sailed across to Greece from the east or the west, has not been determined. We have found no convenient trail marked by abandoned characteristic pottery or artifacts, or even by the bones of horses. Further exploration and excavation in the lower Balkans may yet bring to light new illuminating evidence. In the meantime the problem offers an open field for speculation and conjecture.

CHAPTER VII

Troy VIIa

DÖRPFELD AND HIS COLLEAGUES in their excavations of 1894 discovered that the layer which had previously been ascribed to the Seventh City, or Troy VII, actually consisted of two distinct and separate strata which in several respects differed sharply one from the other. Dörpfeld, who thereupon designated them as VII^1 and VII^2, observed that the former represented a direct unbroken continuation of the culture of Troy VI, while VII^2 was marked by the appearance of new strange elements not heretofore seen on the site. This twofold division was fully confirmed in the excavations conducted by the Cincinnati Expedition, which ventured only to alter the terms VII^1 and VII^2 to VIIa and VIIb. So far as could be determined, Troy VIIa seems to have lived out its whole span of life within a single phase without subdivisions, probably lasting little or no longer than one generation of men.

In the ruins heaped up by the earthquake no traces of human victims were found. It looks as if the inhabitants escaped with their lives, if not with all their possessions. Perhaps it was one of those severe earthquakes that sometimes give warning of their coming by preliminary rumblings. However that may be, it seems safe to conclude that the population survived and it is clear that they immediately set about making the town once again habitable. One of the first tasks was to restore the fortification wall around the citadel. A great deal of the lower part of it, with sloping face, had certainly withstood the violence of the shock, but the superstructure obviously had to be rebuilt.

On the eastern side of the fortress a substantial addition was attached to the southern end of Section 2 of the older wall, which here overlapped the East Gateway. This extension of Period VIIa carried on the line of the fortification southward

Plates 52, 59

Fig. 36

Plate 42

toward the easterly corner of Tower VI h, lengthening considerably the narrow passage that led to the East Gate. Perhaps it was intended to make the approach to the entrance more difficult between the end of the wall and the angle of the tower. But this part of the extension was later destroyed when the deep foundations of a great Roman colonnade, called IX M by Dörpfeld, were laid straight through, effacing the structure of Troy VIIa. Only a section, some 16 m. long, of the new wall thus survived to modern times, and a great part of that was

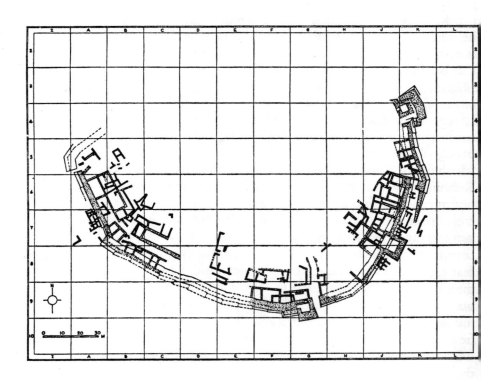

Fig. 36 Diagrammatic plan of buildings of Troy VII

demolished in 1893–94 to facilitate the laying of track for a light railway to carry away the earth and debris excavated along the eastern flank of the hill. What is left of this wall of Troy VIIa is solidly built, but in a style far less regular than that of the Sixth Settlement. It made use of a mixture of materials: many fallen blocks from the earlier wall combined with smaller unworked stones. Perhaps there was need for haste in rehabilitating the defences. In this eastern area the new section may have served in part as a retaining wall, for the passage to the East Gate now evidently ascended considerably; this was necessary since the ground level inside the fortress had been raised as much as 2 m. by the fallen debris, and many of the new houses of Troy VIIa were erected with their floors at that higher level.

Evidence of reconstruction of the great wall may also be observed along the southeast and south sides of the circuit as far as the South Gate. That gate itself was repaired, and it continued to be the principal entrance into the citadel. The passage through the opening was paved with large flat stones which extended more than 3 m. northward into the enclosure. Running down through the middle of the paved area was an underground drain, about 0.40 m. wide and 0.50 m. deep, roofed over with heavy slabs of limestone which had not been worked into uniform shapes. The drain had a floor made of large flat blocks; it was lined with lateral walls built of irregular material, much of which had obviously been salvaged from the fallen wreckage shaken down by the earthquake. The drain was no doubt meant to carry off rain-water from a little plaza, just inside the gateway, on which converging streets descended from the north and west. In a heavy shower a vast quantity of water must have come pouring down from the upper part of the acropolis, flooding the open space before the gate. The stone pavement and the drain were prolonged southward outside the fortress well past the angle of Tower VI i; but how

Plate 60

149

far they once extended cannot now be determined, since the area outside the gate was thoroughly disturbed by the erection of several structures in Hellenistic and Roman times.

Plate 62

Similar damage of the same general date has left us with all too little evidence of what was done in the way of repair and renovation of the fortification wall to the west of Tower VI i. But along its inner side remains of many houses of Settlement VIIa were found, by Dörpfeld and the Cincinnati Expedition, extending as far as the northwestern angle of the citadel. An almost continuous row of small dwellings of this kind was built abutting on the inside face of the wall, which therefore must have been standing or re-erected high enough to form the southern side of each of these buildings. Houses were also discovered on a higher concentric terrace within the outer ring, but Dörpfeld found no traces of buildings of Troy VIIa in the central part of the acropolis and he therefore considered the possibility that there never were any. As shown in his own schematic drawing of the whole mound in cross-section, however, no part of the layers of Troy VIIa, VIIb, and VIII was left in place in the central area after the Hellenistic and Roman levelling of the top of the hill. No doubt the entire citadel was occupied in the time of Troy VIIa, as in the preceding periods, and the residences of the ruler and the leading families must have stood, as heretofore, in the high quarters that dominated the settlement.

Fig. 37

Though we have no idea of the size and plan of the palace or of the abodes of the leaders of the community, the simple habitations of the less wealthy citizens are fairly well represented. They differ conspicuously from the imposing freestanding manorial houses of Troy VI. The walls, though thick and sturdy, were roughly built of heterogeneous material, including a great many squared blocks that were recovered from the debris heaped up by the earthquake. No real effort seems to have been made to render the structures handsome:

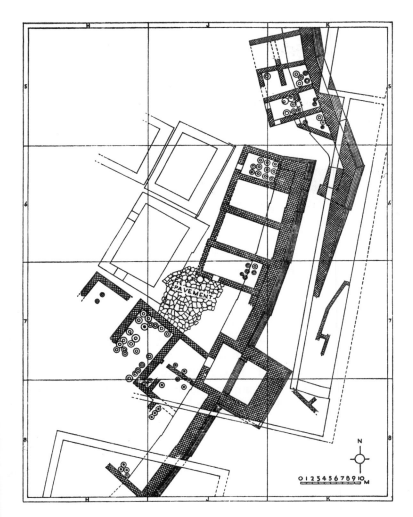

Fig. 37 Plan of houses of Troy VIIa along eastern side of citadel

the work was probably done in the haste born of emergency. These small houses were crowded closely together, often being separated only by party walls, a device which seems not to have been used in Troy VI. Especially noteworthy is the lengthy row of lean-to apartments along the inner side of the circuit wall; some 20 to 30 such houses were compressed into the area between the wall and the lowest terrace of the citadel, a space which in the days of Troy VI had been kept open and perhaps served as a street. On the terrace above, a few of the great houses of the Sixth Settlement were reconstructed and reoccupied, notably Houses VI G and VI M, and possibly the Pillar House in part. Most of the other large buildings had presumably been too severely damaged by the earthquake to be rehabilitated; they were replaced by smaller superposed struc-tures. The latter, too, had been squeezed together, with party walls dividing them into small apartments. It is difficult to avoid the conclusion that the acropolis in Settlement VIIa was obliged to shelter a larger population than its predecessor of Troy VI.

In the eastern quarter of the acropolis, between House VI F and the fortification wall, are remains of a handsome stone pavement made of large flattish slabs. The part preserved is 12 m. long from north to south and 10 m. wide, but it once probably extended toward the east as far as the citadel wall, and westward it continued across the demolished east wall of House VI F. The pavement is a work of Troy VIIa, and it evidently belonged to an open public plaza which gave the populace spacious and relatively dry access to a deep well. The latter had been made and used in the time of Troy VI and the circular shaft was lined with a well-built stone wall. After the earthquake the well was put back into service, two truncated *pithoi* of large size, one set above the other, being installed to raise the lining of the shaft nearly 2 m. to the new ground level. Many of those who lived in the acropolis must have come to this place to fetch water; to accommodate them it was necessary, despite the shortage of space, to leave an adequate approach free of houses. In modern times a wild pear tree has taken root not far from the well, and we like to think that a remote predecessor in the thirteenth century BC offered shade to drawers of water for a quiet gossip at the well.

Settlement VIIa was almost wholly destroyed by fire, and whatever survived that calamity was further damaged by the subsequent reconstruction of Troy VIIb and more particularly by the expanded building programme in Roman times. As a result of these adversities nearly all of the small habitations of Period VIIa were found in a sadly ruined state. No distinctive house plans appear. The dwellings consist of one, two, or three – rarely, if ever, more – small rooms, with no unity of design, no principal façade. Party walls divide buildings into separate habitations of unequal size, resembling refugee quarters for temporary use until better accommodation could be provided. Detailed descriptions of specific examples are unnecessary.

One house, different from almost all the others, perhaps deserves a brief description. That is House 700, the first building on the right when one has passed through the South Gate into the acropolis. Only the western part of the house has survived, the eastern half, or more, having been destroyed when a large Council Chamber was constructed in Roman times. There were certainly three rooms, possibly a fourth. Towards the northern end of the house a wide doorway gave access from the street to a small lobby. Thence a narrow door opposite the first opened eastward into a room which is now missing, while another, wider, doorway led southward to an apartment of considerable size. This contained a central hearth, oval in shape and raised some 0.25 m. above the earth floor. The edge was reinforced by fragments of coarse pottery. Beside the hearth to the south a stone saddle quern had been set in crude brick and clay; it was fixed in a tilted position, so that flour ground upon it would fall into a fairly deep basin-like container, hollowed out in the floor and smoothly lined with clay. The hollow contained carbonised remains of wheat and probably of vetch. Along the western wall was a kitchen 'sink', built of stone and paved with flattish slabs, and connected with a drain that was pierced through the wall to empty into the street. Farther south alongside the wall were remains of two fireboxes with a crude brick shell and filled with charred matter and ashes. They probably formed the lower part of an oven for baking. The southern end of the room was occupied by remains of storage bins, built of crude brick, which contained some remains of carbonised wheat. The equipment of this room suggests that House 700, besides serving as a dwelling, was also a bakery or a cookshop, where travellers passing in or out of the citadel might stop for refreshments. Perhaps it was a 'snack bar', one of the earliest known.

The house walls of Troy VIIa, which had been built largely of blocks quarried from the debris of the Sixth Settlement, were found still standing in not a few places to a height of 1 to 2 m., and in a good many instances the floors, made of hard-packed earth or clay, had escaped serious damage. When exposed they revealed a remarkable peculiarity, which may unquestionably be taken as a distinctive feature of Troy VIIa; this is the presence in almost every house of large *pithoi*, or storage jars, which had been set so deep into the ground that only the rim appeared at the level of the floor, where it was covered with a heavy stone slab. Varying considerably in size, these capacious jars range from 1.75 to 2 m. in height and from 1 to 1.25 m. in diameter. Some houses contained only one or two *pithoi*, but there were usually more, numbering from four or five to a dozen and, in one instance, House 731, reaching a full score. In several rooms the whole floor was honeycombed with these deep-set jars, but the stone lids made it possible to walk freely about the chamber and to utilise all the floor space. In one or two buildings, however, it was obvious that the floors, undermined by so many cavities, had collapsed or given

Plate 61

Plate 63
Fig. 38

way, necessitating along with the replacement of some broken *pithoi* the making of a new floor. When the deep holes to accommodate these big jars were dug by the householders some intrusive elements naturally found their way into the stratum of wreckage piled up by the earthquake. It was not always easy in excavating to differentiate all of the intrusive items.

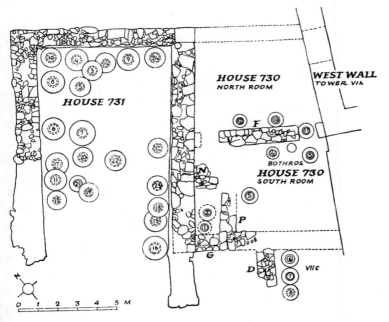

Fig. 38 Plan of Houses 730 and 731 containing many pithoi, Troy VIIa

In all the layers of the settlements belonging to the Early Bronze Age and also in the deposits of Troy VI evidence has come to light showing that *pithoi* were regularly used and in considerable numbers, for the storage of solid as well as liquid supplies. Most often the vessels stood on the floor, though they were sometimes set in relatively shallow hollows cut into the ground to serve as sockets. But it was not until the period of Settlement VIIa that the jars were sunk to their full height beneath the floor. This innovation was probably introduced to provide the maximum possible capacity for the storage of food and drink, while at the same time leaving free the entire floor area inside these rather small habitations. It seems to me that we are justified in interpreting this evidence as confirming the view that the acropolis was now crowded with people and that space within the walls was at a premium; I think one may also deduce further that there was an emer, gency of some kind.

A part from the architectural remains which, though sadly incomplete, shed useful light on the prompt efforts made by the inhabitants to rebuild the settlement after the earthquake, the layer of Troy VIIa yielded relatively little of intrinsic value or of artistic merit. Alfred Götze, who studied all the miscel, laneous objects that were recovered in the excavations of 1893– 94 and who wrote the final report on them, found the artifacts from the latest phases of the Sixth Settlement and from Troy VIIa so nearly identical that they could not be surely differen, tiated. The Cincinnati Expedition was able to isolate and keep segregated a number of closed groups of objects from strata that were assignable to the two periods mentioned and could be guaranteed as free from intrusions; but here again the same difficulty was encountered: for no real difference could be perceived. The miscellaneous objects from Troy VIIa are less numerous than those from earlier periods. The wholly un, contaminated deposits left were not very abundant, often small, and not rich in their yield of material. Such as it was, however, it demonstrates that there was no cultural break between Troy VI and Troy VIIa.

A comparison of the pottery from the same two layers and periods confirms this conclusion. As pointed out by Schmidt,

Plate 64

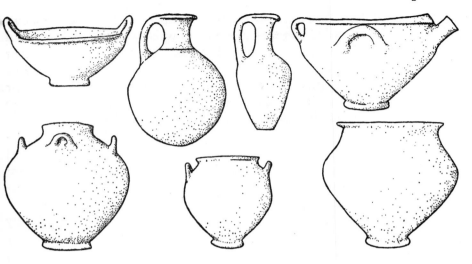

Fig. 39 Characteristic pottery shapes of Troy VIIa

who worked over all the sherds and pots unearthed in the
digging campaigns of 1890, 1893 and 1894, and who pub‑
lished the catalogue of the Schliemann Collection, the pottery
of Troy VIIa is indistinguishable from that of Troy VI (in its
final phase, VIh). For this reason Schmidt, in *Troja und Ilion*
as well as in the catalogue of the Collection, dealt with the
pottery of Troy VI and VIIa all together as a single insepar‑
able unit.

The same problem confronted the Cincinnati Expedition.
In Troy VIIa, Grey Minyan Ware occurs in profusion in the
identical characteristic fabric, finish and shapes that prevailed
in Phase VIh. Tan Ware too appears in the same types of
vessels, with the same slip or finishing coat, and the same
incised and plastic decoration that had distinguished it in the
closing years of the Sixth Settlement. One special variety of
Tan Ware which first made its appearance before the end of

Fig. 39

157

Troy VI becomes highly characteristic of Period VIIa, and this ware is of some importance when we come to the problem of dating the settlement. If we seem to have overemphasised the fact of the continuity of culture transmitted from Troy VI to VIIa, it is because there has been some misunderstanding of the close connection between the two periods and the substantial survival of the population into Troy VIIa.

Fig. 40 Examples of Mycenaean Ware found in deposits of Troy VIIa

Mycenaean pottery continued to be used in the settlement that rose up again after the earthquake. If the fragments found by the Cincinnati Expedition may be taken as representative, there seems to have been a falling-off in the quantity of imported vessels as compared with locally produced imitations: 90 sherds of the former class were recovered from uncontaminated deposits as against more than 250 fragments of adaptations presumably made at Troy. The imported pieces belong to the categories which Furumark called Mycenaean III A and III B, the majority falling in the latter class. It is particularly worth noting, however, that a good many pots in the distinctive Tan Ware of Troy VIIa mentioned above were decorated with patterns copied or adapted from motifs that were characteristic of the Mycenaean III A style. It is therefore clear that Settlement VIIa was already in existence at a time when Mycenaean pottery of the III A class was still being made and used. Among the Mycenaean sherds recovered from undisturbed deposits of Troy VIIa no certain examples attributable in shape or decoration to Furumark's category of Mycenaean III C were recognised by the Cincinnati Expedition. Settlement VIIa must therefore have come to its end before the Mycenaean III C style had been introduced, and indeed probably long before that time, while pottery of Mycenaean III A was still in common use. We are consequently able, at least approximately, to fit the life span of Settlement VIIa into the background formed by the now established and accepted sequence of Mycenaean ceramic styles.

In a thorough, searching study of Mycenaean pottery Furumark has worked out so far as is yet possible the absolute chronology of the many characteristic styles that followed, one after the other, from the sixteenth to the end of the twelfth century B C. For the later part of this period he has differentiated three categories: Mycenaean III A, III B, and III C, the first and third having several minor subdivisions. Taking into

Fig. 40

consideration all the evidence available – chiefly the synchron
isms that can be established by comparison and correlation o
Mycenaean objects found in datable Egyptian contexts and o
Egyptian objects recovered in observed Mycenaean stratigraphi
associations – he reached the conclusion that the style o
Mycenaean III A prevailed from about 1425 to 1300 B C, tha
of III B from 1300 to 1230 B C and that of III C from 123
to 1100 B C. These datings were of course meant only a
approximations. Though there are some minor disagreement
in detail – inevitable, since the evidence itself is at best some
what tenuous and conflicting – most field archaeologists accep
these dates in general, sometimes rounding them out for con
venience and simplicity into whole centuries, the fourteent
century for Mycenaean III A, the thirteenth for III B, and th
twelfth for III C.

In accordance with Furumark's chronology, the change i
ceramic style from III A to III B worked itself out about 130
B C, and this must give us the approximate date of the earth
quake that ruined the walls and houses of the Sixth Settlement
it also fixes the start of the reconstruction that followed withi
a few days of that catastrophe, and which we take as marking
the beginning of Troy VIIa. The time of that settlement's end
too, can be calculated, if not exactly, at any rate without grea
inaccuracy. The habitation deposit of Troy VIIa consisted o
a single stratum and there is nothing to indicate that it repre
sents a lengthy span of life. It may have lasted a full generation,
or half a century at most, but it was probably of considerabl
shorter duration. The associated Mycenaean pottery include
many fragments with painted decoration in the style of Myce
naean III A, although the greater part belongs to the early
stages of III B; the Grey Minyan Ware, moreover, differs littl
if at all from that of Phase VIh. The overthrow of Settlemen
VIIa must surely have been brought about by 1250 B C, if no
a decade or two earlier.

Whatever the precise date, the destruction was undoubtedly the work of human agency, and it was accompanied by violence and by fire. A great mass of stones and crude brick, along with other burned and blackened debris, was heaped up over the ruined houses as well as in the streets, and once again the ground level rose appreciably. Amid the wreckage in House 700 – the first on the right inside the South Gate – were found fragments of a human skull; other bits, collected in the street outside the house, may have belonged to the same individual. Pieces of another cranium were uncovered farther to the westward in Street 711. A lower jaw-bone, probably of an adult male, was found outside the eastern fortification wall in the burnt stratum on the floor of House 741. On the western slope of the hill outside the acropolis wall, at the top of a stratum that produced pottery like that of Troy VIh and VIIa, a skeleton was found. The bones, though still more or less held together, seemed not to lie in the normal manner of a proper burial: it looked rather as if the man had been struck down there and, left as he fell, been covered by debris from above. The skull had been crushed and the lower jaw broken away. Were these the remains of a victim, either an attacker or a defender, who was killed in the struggle that preceded the capture of the town ? It is by no means improbable; indeed, it is highly probable. But we cannot answer the question with certainty.

In any event the cumulative evidence seems to me to be sufficient to demonstrate that fighting and killing must have accompanied the destruction of Troy VIIa. The crowding together of numerous small houses everywhere that space could be found indicates that shelter had to be provided within the fortification walls for a greatly increased population; and the installation of innumerable capacious storage jars beneath the floor in almost every house and room points to the necessity for laying up as much as possible in the way of supplies of food and drink for an emergency. What could it mean other than a siege by invading hostile forces? The fire-blackened wreckage and ruins of the settlement offer a vivid picture of the harsh fate that was regularly meted out to a town besieged, captured and looted by implacable enemies, as is so graphically described in the accounts of marauding expeditions in the Homeric poems, when the men were ruthlessly slain and the women and children carried off into slavery.

Here, then, in the extreme northwestern corner of Asia Minor – exactly where Greek tradition, folk memory and the epic poems place the site of Ilios – we have the physical remains of a fortified stronghold, obviously the capital of the region. As shown by persuasive archaeological evidence, it was besieged and captured by enemies and destroyed by fire, no doubt after having been thoroughly pillaged, just as Hellenic poetry and folk-tale describe the destruction of King Priam's Troy.

For a long time most historians and archaeologists have more or less tacitly accepted as the date for the fall of Troy the year 1184 BC, a date fixed by the calculations of Eratosthenes, a scholar of wide learning in many fields of knowledge, who lived and worked chiefly in the second half of the third century BC in Alexandria. He based his chronological computations mainly on the study of the genealogies of the Spartan kings and others, by means of which he reached back 328 years before the First Olympiad (776 BC) to the year 1104 BC for the Dorian Invasion. Greek tradition reckoned this event as occurring two generations after the fall of Troy. The latter, with an allowance of 40 years to a generation, or 80 years earlier all told, was thus put back to 1184 BC. Other ancient historians and chronographers – and there were many – had also worked out the problem from the same evidence, but with variant genealogies and/or with different estimates for the average length of a generation. Their conjectures range over a span of two centuries for this crucial date, from 1334 (Douris of Samos) to 1135 BC (Ephoros of Kyme in Aeolis), with numerous inter-mediate guesses.

It is obvious therefore that there was no sacred, inviolable, established date for the taking of Troy, nor is there – in the variable make-up of the genealogical lists – any immutably fixed absolute date for the Dorian Invasion. In view of these circumstances the archaeological testimony must surely be recognised as much more reliable than that of tradition and conjecture. On the evidence of the Mycenaean pottery (found in the habitation deposit of the burned settlement) which can be dated in conformity with Furumark's ceramic chronology, Troy VIIa was destroyed appreciably before the middle of the thirteenth century, that is to say about 1260 BC, if not indeed somewhat earlier.

This conclusion is firmly supported by the results of archaeo-logical researches during the past dozen years or more, which have made it clear that almost all the major Mycenaean sites on the Greek mainland – except possibly in Attica – were reduced to ruins toward, or at the end of, the ceramic phase III B. Mycenae, Tiryns, Pylos, Gla, and, almost certainly, Thebes were consumed by fire, and most of the smaller settle-ments, such as Berbati, Prosymna, and Zygouries, to mention only a few, suffered the same fate and were abandoned. By or before 1200 BC, therefore, the power of the Mycenaean main-land was shattered; the great centres that are recorded in the Catalogue of Ships as having contributed the chief contingents to the expedition against Troy under Agamemnon, lay deserted or dilapidated, the remaining inhabitants facing a harsh struggle for survival. The period when pottery in the style of III C was being made and was in general use was one of poverty and decay, and the great days of Mycenaean glory were only a memory. That was not the time when a mighty coalition of Mycenaean kings and princes could be formed to undertake an ambitious and risky overseas war of conquest. That enterprise must have been carried out much earlier when the Mycenaean world was at the height of its political, economic, and military strength, and the imposing royal palaces stood in their grandeur offering gracious hospitality to welcome guests. This was before the first half of the thirteenth century had reached its end, when Mycenaean pottery in an early stage of the III B style prevailed along with survivals of the III A class in the citadel of Troy VIIa, at the time when this citadel was taken by force and put to the torch.

It is Settlement VIIa, then, that must be recognised as the actual Troy, the ill-fated stronghold, the siege and capture of which caught the fancy and imagination of contemporary troubadours and bards who transmitted orally to their successors their songs about the heroes who fought in the war. There were no doubt many additions as well as excisions of incident or detail from time to time in the long course of transmission until in the hands of a poetic genius the various separate lays were fused together into the epics that have come down to us.

CHAPTER VIII

Troy VIIb

MANY OF THE INHABITANTS evidently survived the destruction of Settlement VIIa, and once again – no doubt soon after the raiders had departed – the citadel was reoccupied. The blackened debris left by the fire was heaped up everywhere to a height ranging from 0.50 m. to more than 1 m. above the former ground level, and the new houses were superposed over the ruins of their predecessors. But the builders seem to have been familiar with the earlier state of affairs, for the new structures were usually founded on the stumps of the walls that had belonged to the older houses, and they followed the same general plans.

Fig. 4

Hubert Schmidt in 1894 observed that the lowest stratum of Troy VIIb contained many fragments of Grey Minyan and Tan Wares almost indistinguishable from those that were characteristic of Settlements VIIa and VI; while in the upper levels these types had for the most part been displaced by a new kind of pottery, Knobbed Ware, hitherto unknown at Troy. This observation was fully confirmed by the excavations in the 1930's, and it is clear that Troy VIIb passed through two distinct phases or periods. They have been called Troy VIIb 1 and Troy VIIb 2 respectively, and these terms may be applied both to the periods and to the corresponding accumulated deposits of habitation rubbish. Each phase has left a layer of debris ranging from 0.75 m. to 1.50 m. and more in thickness. In many sectors of the excavation the division between the two strata was clearly visible, but in some places no sharp cleavage could be detected.

Nothing much need be said regarding the character of Settlement VIIb 1 since it obviously represents a direct survival of the culture that prevailed in Troy VIIa. The fortification wall

TROY
VIIb 1

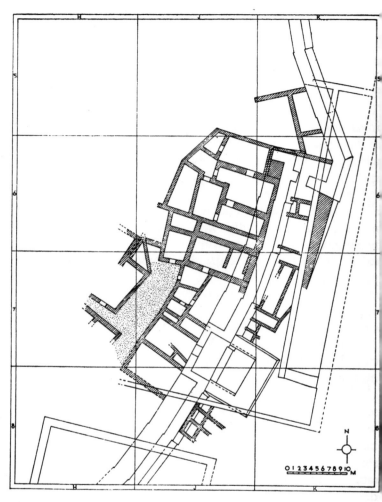

Fig. 41 *Plan of buildings of Troy VIIb along eastern side of the citadel*

evidently still continued to stand, or was repaired, to a sufficient
height for the small houses abutting on its inner face to be rebuilt. The East Gate may have been closed altogether, but
the South Gate was renovated and still served as the principal

entrance to the citadel. The main street leading straight to the upper part of the acropolis followed the line of its forerunner; it had a substantial pavement of fairly large rough stones that lay 0.90 m. above the top of the cover slabs of the drain of Troy VIIa. The pavement was preserved to a length of 7 m. inside the gate. The street of the preceding period, branching at right angles toward the west, was likewise rehabilitated along with the habitations on each side of it. Dörpfeld thought it likely that similar houses rose up throughout the acropolis.

Miscellaneous objects recovered from certified uncontaminated strata are too few to shed much light on conditions of life in Phase VIIb 1; but such as they are, they suggest that there was little change of any consequence from the preceding period, except possibly that there was now greater poverty. As for the pottery, Grey Minyan and Tan Wares still retain their dominant position with hardly any perceptible alteration; but one or two minor innovations may be noted in details, such, for example, as a new sharpness in the modelling of ringbases.

How Settlement VIIb 1 came to its end is an unsolved mystery. The circuit wall apparently stood undamaged, as it had been before. There is no sign of destruction whether by earthquake or by human hands or in any other manner: the houses seem to have been taken over and occupied by the new masters without serious disturbance. The newcomers enlarged the buildings by adding on rooms in various directions, wherever space was available; and they joined together many of the earlier singleroomed dwellings by opening communicating doorways through former party walls. The East Gate was now certainly closed to traffic, being blocked by a house built directly across the passage. The South Gate, however, survived as well as the roadway leading to the upper central part of the citadel. This street, too, was provided with a pavement of irregular stone slabs, which were laid on a bed of small stones and pebbles. The surface now rose to a level of 0.50 m. to

0.65 m. above the earlier road of Troy VIIb 1. The branch
street running westward, parallel to the fortification, likewise
continued to be used.

In almost all the new constructions and repairs the people
of Troy VIIb 2 introduced a novel architectural feature by
setting a row of irregular orthostate slabs of no great size in the
face and in the lower part of a wall, at or just below ground
level. This useful criterion for dating a building to Settlement
VIIb 2 was first noted by Dörpfeld. Orthostates had occasionally made their appearance in a few instances in earlier periods,
but their general and almost regular use is distinctive of Troy
VIIb 2.

Miscellaneous objects of metal, stone, bone, horn, and other
materials from stratified deposits of Troy VIIb 2 were disappointingly few; for the houses that had stood in the central
part of the citadel were all demolished and removed in Roman
times, and the only remains to survive lay along the lower edge
of the acropolis, inside and outside the fortification wall of the
Sixth Settlement. As we have seen, this was a belt that had
also suffered particular damage from later intrusions and depredations. So far as could be judged, the miscellaneous items of
Troy VIIb 2 are – with a few exceptions – much like those
of Periods VIIb 1 and VIIa.

Several bronze implements – a double axe (or perhaps a
mattock), two hammeraxes, a socketed pointed punch (or
pointed hammer), and moulds for a socketed axe, a socketed
celt, and a flat celt, all resembling wellknown Hungarian
types, – were, however, found by Schliemann at Troy. All are
of unrecorded stratigraphic provenience, but it has usually been
assumed – and with great plausibility – that they must be
contemporary with the Knobbed Ware that is distinctive of
Troy VIIb 2.

Another exception is a terracotta figurine, remarkable for
its grotesqueness and the careless manner in which it was

Plate 65

Plate 66

Plate 66

made. It looks almost like a caricature of a human female, and it has no antecedents on the Trojan hill. It must be the product of an initial, unschooled stage of modelling in clay; but no comparable piece seems to have been found at any other site either near-by or distant. The figurine appears to fit reasonably well into the cultural background that created what has been called Knobbed Ware.

The latter which is notably characteristic of Phase VIIb 2, is all hand-made – a strange phenomenon to appear suddenly on a site where the potter's wheel has been familiar for many centuries. With its crude, irregular unsymmetrical forms and its startling projections, decorative knobs, or horns, that show no little power of invention, this kind of pottery looks highly primitive, or at least backward. It occurs in more than a dozen different shapes none of which is known from any of the earlier periods on the site of Troy. These pots ranging from black to brown or grey and even lighter hues, with highly polished and usually lustrous surface, are not without a certain attractiveness of their own.

Fig. 42

Plate 67

Before leaving the subject of pottery we must take note of the fact that alongside the Knobbed Ware, which is predominant, Grey Minyan and Tan Ware still continue to be made and used in appreciable quantities on the site. This survival implies that a part, at least, of the earlier population must have lingered on in Settlement VIIb 2.

Knobbed Ware was long ago recognised as showing an unmistakable general kinship with fabrics that have been found in deposits of the Late Bronze Age in Hungary. This connection linking Troy VIIb 2 and the valley of the Danube strengthened the probability that the bronze implements mentioned above, despite their lack of a recorded place of discovery, might safely be attributed to the same settlement. As pointed out by K. Bittel, however, a comparative study of the objects themselves reveals considerable differences between the

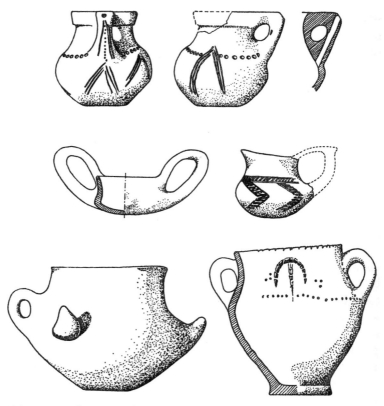

Fig. 42 Some characteristic shapes of Knobbed Ware, Troy VIIb

two areas; they are especially noticeable in the shapes of the pottery and in other details, and Bittel concludes that a direct connection between Troy and the Hungarian plain cannot safely be postulated. As suggested previously by Schmidt, the invaders may well have come from Thrace, where the Danubian culture could have established a foothold at a much earlier period and could have continued developing along new lines of its own. Thrace still remains little known on the archaeological side, but further explorations may shed light on the problem. It is, in any event, hazardous to base on the evidence hitherto available any close synchronisms between Hungary and the Troad.

But it seems obvious that the people who seized control of the Trojan citadel from their predecessors of Settlement VIIb 1 came from across the Hellespont. Their custom of building with the use of orthostates in the walls, their hand, made pottery with its knobbed decoration, and their bronze implements of novel types seem not to have penetrated farther into Asia Minor. There is no evidence that their invasion was an overland movement from the east or south. Nor has any trace of these people yet been found across the Aegean in the Helladic peninsula.

The duration of the two establishments VIIb 1 and VIIb 2 cannot be determined with precision. The depth of the deposit left by each does not by itself settle the matter, although it seems to indicate that each lasted somewhat longer than Troy VIIa, and that Settlement VIIb 1 probably had a shorter life than its successor, which in several places showed traces of two building periods. Although the material is relatively scanty and consists almost exclusively of unrelated sherds, the Mycenaean pottery found in the two layers provides evidence that is of some help. In Period VIIb 1 fragments representing the style of Mycenaean III B still occur in association with a considerably greater number belonging to the III C class. The deposits of Period VIIb 2 also yielded some Mycenaean ware, for the greater part locally made, with very few pieces that could be regarded as from imported pots. The decoration, so far as can be recog, nised, seems to be assignable to the III C category. No examples of Protogeometric or later wares came to light in the context of Troy VIIb 2.

In the present state of our knowledge, it seems safe to draw the conclusion that Settlement VIIb 1 lasted from about 1260 to 1200 BC or shortly thereafter, and Settlement VIIb 2 from then to the close of the twelfth century, 1100 BC, or possibly a decade or two later. Evidence of burning in several houses of Troy VIIb 2 indicates almost certainly that the settlement was destroyed by fire: once again the citadel was evidently captured, looted and put to the torch, this time in the troublous period that throughout the eastern Mediterranean marked the transition from the Late Bronze Age to the Age of Iron.

This new destruction signals the end of ancient Troy and the Trojans. There were undoubtedly on this occasion, too, a good many survivors, but it is clear that they did not reoccupy the hill of Troy. Perhaps it was considered prudent to remove the entire population to a site farther inland, more remote from the sea, and more easily defended. It is tempting to conjecture that it was a considerable body of displaced Trojans who at this time took refuge on the lofty summit of Balli Dagh which rises high above the gorge through which the river Scamander emerges from the mountains into the plain of Troy. Whoever they were, these people carried with them the tradition of making Grey Minyan pottery and maintained it down to the end of the eighth century; around that time the new site was in its turn abandoned. Did some of the inhabitants perhaps then return to Troy? Though there is nothing to prove this, we do know that in the seventh century BC the Trojan citadel, which had been virtually deserted for some four centuries, suddenly blossomed into life once more with occupants who were still able to make Grey Minyan pottery. But the new settlement which was predominantly a Greek colony turned its face toward the west and formed part of the Hellenic world.

Plate 3

Chronology

THE CHRONOLOGY adopted in this volume is summar-
ised in the accompanying table. The dates given, which
make no claim to represent more than a general approximation,
with a wide margin of error in each direction, follow in all
essentials the conclusions reached by the Cincinnati Expedition. These results have been accepted by some scholars but
rejected to a greater or less extent by others, especially by the
advocates of the so-called short chronology. Little, if any, cogent new archaeological evidence has been adduced to impose
a change of view. Those who have worked through many
seasons at Hissarlik in the shadow of the enormously deep
deposits of habitation debris and who have become familiar
with the almost interminable sequence of major and minor
building levels have not been converted to a new faith in the
compressed short chronology.

It was long ago argued that the gold jewellery found by
Schliemann in the 'Great Treasure' – assignable to the final
stage of Troy II – is, if not actually contemporary, a close
forerunner of the ornaments from the Royal Shaft Graves at
Mycenae. At Troy the stratum of Phase IIg – from which the
'treasure' certainly came – is separated from Stratum VId – in
which Mycenaean pottery of LH I, contemporary with the
Shaft Graves, makes its first appearance – by accumulations
more than 8 m. deep, which show 16 distinctly marked inter-
vening levels; most of them represent phases during which
houses were built, occupied, and ultimately destroyed. At a
conservative estimate these phases might well correspond to an
equal – if not greater – number of generations that must have
extended through five or six or more centuries.

Sites on the Greek mainland, too, when they were not 'telescoped' and largely cut away to make room for great structures – for example, those at Eutresis and Lerna – have revealed similar deep accumulations of rubbish and ruins, with multiple stratigraphic subdivisions that speak convincingly of long periods of human occupation.

A general chronology cannot safely be worked out from the evidence of any one site alone. It must be based on the results obtained at many sites, with due allowance for local accidents and vicissitudes. The large establishments often afford a less trustworthy record than more modest settlements, which sometimes escaped the disturbance caused by grading, changing of levels, and deep digging for the foundations of palaces and great structures. Whole underlying layers could easily be eliminated by ambitious works in later times, as well illustrated in the central part of the citadel at Troy itself.

In any event, it seems to me as reasonable still to hold firmly to a relatively long chronology for the Early and Middle Bronze Age.

Chronological Table

Troy I	3000–2500 B C
II	2500–2200
III	2200–2050
IV	2050–1900
V	1900–1800
VI	1800–1300
VIIa	1300–1260
VIIb 1	1260–1190
VIIb 2	1190–1100
VIII	700–

Selected Bibliography

BITTEL, K.: *Prähistorische Forschung in Kleinasien* (Istanbuler Forschungen, Vol. VI). Istanbul, 1934.
Kleinasiatische Studien (Istanbuler Mitteilungen, No. 5). Istanbul, 1942.
Grundzüge der Vor- und Frühgeschichte Kleinasiens, 2nd ed. Tübingen, 1950.

BLEGEN, C. W., BOULTER, C. G., CASKEY, J. L., RAWSON, M., and SPERLING, J.: *Troy: Excavations Conducted by the University of Cincinnati, 1932–38*, 4 vols. Princeton, 1950–58.

BOSSERT, H.: *Altanatolien: Kunst und Handwerk in Kleinasien von den Anfängen bis zum völligen Aufgeben in der griechischen Kultur.* Berlin, 1942.

CHEVALIER: *Description of the Plain of Troy.* Edinburgh, 1791. (For the French edition see Lechevalier.)

DÖRPFELD, W.: *Bericht über die im Jahre 1893 in Troja veranstalteten Ausgrabungen.* Leipzig, 1894.
Troja und Ilion: Ergebnisse der Ausgrabungen in den vorhistorischen und historischen Schichten von Ilion, 1870–94. Athens, 1902.

FURUMARK, A.: *The Mycenaean Pottery Analysis and Classification.* Stockholm, 1941.
The Chronology of Mycenaean Pottery. Stockholm, 1941.

LAMB, W.: *Excavations at Thermi in Lesbos.* Cambridge, 1936.

LEAF, W.: *Troy: A Study in Homeric Geography.* London, 1912.
Homer and History. London, 1915.

LECHEVALIER, J. B.: *Voyage de la Troade fait 1785–86.* 3 vols. Paris, 1802.
Recueille de Cartes, Plans, Vues et Médailles pour servir au Voyage de la Troade. Paris, 1802.

MACLAREN, C.: *Dissertation on the Topography of the Plain of Troy.* Edinburgh, 1822.

MATZ, FR.: *Kreta, Mykene, Troja, die minoische und die homerische Welt.* 2nd ed., Stuttgart, 1956.

NILSSON, M. P.: *The Mycenaean Origin of Greek Mythology.* Berkeley, 1932.

PAGE, D.: *History and the Homeric Iliad.* Berkeley, 1959.

SCHACHERMEYR, FR.: *Die ältesten Kulturen Griechenlands.* Stuttgart, 1955. *Prähistorische Kulturen Griechenlands* (Pauly-Wissowa-Kroll, Vol. 22). Stuttgart, 1954.

SCHLIEMANN, H.: *Ithaka, der Peloponnes und Troja.* Leipzig, 1869. *Troy and its Remains.* London, 1875. *Ilios the City and Country of the Trojans.* London, 1880. *Troja: Results of the Latest Researches and Discoveries on the Site of Homer's Troy.* London, 1884. *Bericht über die Ausgrabungen in Troja im Jahre 1890.* Leipzig, 1891.

SCHMIDT, H.: *Heinrich Schliemann's Sammlung Trojanischer Altertümer.* Berlin, 1902.

SCHUCHHARDT, C.: *Schliemann's Excavations* (English translation by E. Sellers). London, 1892.

VENTRIS, M. G. F., and CHADWICK, J.: *Documents in Mycenaean Greek.* Cambridge, 1956.

Notes on the Plates

1 The steep northern slope of the mound of Troy as seen from the plain of the Dumbrek Su, the river usually identified as the Simoeis.

2 The northern edge of the hill as seen from the east, with mounds of earth from the excavations.

3 The high cliff called Balli Dagh rising precipitately above the Scamander River.

4 Professor W. T. Semple, Dr Wilhelm Dörpfeld and Mrs Semple outside the excavation house at Troy in 1935.

5 Pinnacle in Square E 6 left by Schliemann and Dörpfeld, and excavated by the Cincinnati Expedition.

6 Pinnacle in Square F 4–5, left by Schliemann; part of it was excavated by the Cincinnati Expedition.

7 Schliemann's great North-South Trench as it looked in 1938. From the south.

8 Fortification wall and east side of tower flanking the South Gate in the middle period of Troy I. From northeast.

9 South face of the tower, and the wall beyond, with its appreciable batter. Middle stage of Troy I. From southwest.

10 Fortification wall of Late Period of Troy I on north side of citadel. Above this wall, at upper left, appears the bottom of the fortification wall of Troy II. From northeast.

11 House-wall of Early Troy I neatly built of small stones laid in a distinctive herring-bone style of masonry.

12 Apsidal house of Phase Ia, lying underneath a larger building of Phase Ib. Whether the apse was roofed or open to the sky is uncertain.

13 House of *megaron* type, Phase Ib, consisting of a single large room with a porch facing westwards. From east.

14 Large jar containing bones of an infant buried just outside House 102. Phase Ib.

15 Typical objects and artifacts found in layer of Troy I. Four daggers or knives made from ribs of oxen; seven bird-bones each with string-hole at one end, forming a necklace; copper fishhook without barb; five awls and pins of bone; two fangs of dogs, pierced for stringing; stone pendant; three whorls or buttons of terracotta; at left, five marble figurines or idols; crude terracotta figurine.

16 Fragments of rims of bowls, Troy I, with moulded and incised representations of human faces; four examples of characteristic horizontal tubular lugs, plain, fluted, or with incised decoration.

17 Heart-shaped human face represented in low relief on a stone stele, perhaps from a shrine, or a memorial monument or a tomb.

18 Skeleton of a child about 11 years old, buried in flexed position on its left side just outside fortification wall of Middle I.

19 Fortification wall built in third phase of Troy II to northwest of gateway approached by great paved ramp, as it appeared in 1894.

20 Stone base for a wooden column that supported roof over colonnade bordering court in front of *megaron* of Phase IIc.

21 Ramp paved with great limestone slabs leading up to southwestern gateway, built in Troy IIc; as it appeared in 1937. From south.

22 Floor of Room 202 covered with fallen pots and other objects which were abandoned by the occupants of the house who fled when fire swept over the settlement.

23 Gold sauceboat found by Schliemann in the 'Great Treasure'. It has a shallow spout at each end and a high handle on each side. The hollow handles were attached to the vessel by soldering.

24 The smaller of the two famous diadems from the 'Great Treasure' found by Schliemann. It was made up of 1750 flat ring-like gold beads, forming the chains, and 354 leaves and pendants.

25 Royal battle-axes from Schliemann's Treasure L, probably of last phase of Troy II. The one shown top left is made of bluish stone, similar to lapis lazuli, the others of dark greenish nephrite.

26 Distinctive objects of Troy II. Crystal pendant and crystal lion's head; two marble idols; copper knife with upturned point; spool-shaped pestle of variegated marble, possibly of Early Cycladic or Early Helladic origin; silver bowl and silver tweezers of Phase IId; piece of bone inlay ornamented with incised concentric circles; two bone pins; bone dart or arrow point, once barbed; bone comb; hammer-axe and fragment of another; whetstone; four idols, two of bone and two of stone.

27 Representative pottery of Troy II. Cylindrical goblet with two handles, Schliemann's *depas amphikypellon*; sherd of a red plate bearing crude incised sketch of an armed warrior with helmet and leather corselet; ring vase with spout; three-legged jar; flaring bowl (profile and underside); lid and sherds of face pots.

28 Burial of a child, probably male, 12 or 13 years old, with long narrow skull, interred in contracted position, *c.* 0.40 m. below the floor of Room 201, belonging to Phase IIg.

29 Northeast wall of House 301 built of stone to its full height. Slight traces of a blocked doorway that once led to an adjoining room.

30 Miscellaneous objects of Troy III: two huge limestone idols and a smaller one in marble: fragments of two diadems of bone and a strip of bone inlay, all decorated with incised dotted circles; four tubes of bone, perhaps handles; a figurine and bead of bone; human figure rudely carved from horn of deer.

31 Pots and lids decorated with human faces in relief: two necks of deep jars; a large deep jar with a high neck, shown with a lid placed over it; fragments of two lids, one both in frontal view and in profile. All these are characteristic of Troy III.

32 Pottery of Troy IV. Two face pots, one shown both with frontal view of face and in profile. Below is a low cylindrical lid with projecting flange around upper edge: the top is decorated in incised technique, divided by triple parallel lines (enclosing zigzags) into four quarters, each containing a simple pattern. Note the crossed circle, the swastika, and the rectangular animal with broad branching antlers.

33 Some objects from the layer of Troy IV. Three idols of white marble; two thin slender figurines—or pins or knives (sometimes called razors)— of copper or bronze; two figurines of bone; a sturdy handle cut from deer horn, including part of a branch antler: it is generously decorated with rows of incised dotted circles, and was perhaps used as the handle of a dagger or knife; figurine made from a potsherd.

34 Raised circular hearth with simple open cooking-stand designed to hold a pot over a charcoal fire. Two flat blocks of clay served as stands to support auxiliary vessels near the fire.

35 Table, work-bench or seat in southwestern corner of Room 501. It was made of clay, crude brick and stone, the surface coated with whitewash.

36 Some objects from the layer of Troy V. Thin knife blade of copper or bronze with one cutting edge much worn by use; flint arrowhead neatly shaped with barbs; figurine, shaped like a cricket bat, decorated with incised parallel lines and groups of circles each enclosing a dot; whetstone, pierced for hanging up; spindle-like spool or reel of bone; idol made from rib of an ox; stone idol of headless type with owl-like face.

37 Face pots still occur in Troy V and cylindrical lids with conventional human features. Shallow bowls bearing on the interior a large cross in red paint are popular and also spiral ornaments attached to handles.

38 East fortification wall and tower of Late Troy VI, as they appeared in 1938. From south.

39 The huge tower, VIg, forming the northeastern corner of the citadel in Late VI. From northeast.

40 The northeastern tower, VIg, as exposed by Dörpfeld in 1892.

41 Section 2 of East Fortification Wall as uncovered by Dörpfeld in 1894. Roman foundation at extreme right.

42 Entrance passage leading to East Gate, as exposed in 1932. Section 2 of wall at left, section 3 at right. From north.

43 Detail of fortification wall of Late VI, to west of the South Gate: this imposing elegant style of masonry originally continued more than 120 m. along the whole extent of Section 4.

44 East fortification wall: section 3 at left, section 2 at right. Roman foun-dation between the two. Extension of wall of Troy VIIa in foreground at right. View from south, taken in 1894.

45 Outer face of Tower VIi flanking the South Gate, with row of mono-lithic pillars backed against the tower. From southeast.

46 Fortification wall of Troy VI: in middle ground at right is the west end of Section 4, at left the wall blocking Gate VI U; in foreground, stepped foundation of seats in a Roman theatral area; high in background in centre, the terrace wall supporting House VI M.

47 The South Gate, the chief entrance to the acropolis in Late VI, as re-vealed in 1937.

48 Northwestern section (6) of fortification wall, forming westernmost angle of the citadel; built in same grandiose sytle as Section 4, but suffered much from use as a stone quarry in Hellenistic Roman times.

49 Northeasterly part of House VI G with stone base for a wooden column set on clay floor. From south.

50 One of the largest buildings of Late Troy VI: the Pillar House, so called from the pyramidal pier of stone blocks still standing in the longitudinal axis of the structure. Seen from west in 1937.

51 Minor objects of Troy VI illustrated here include thin bronze knives, barbed arrowheads and a spatula also of bronze; a pendant of nephrite or jadeite in the form of a bird; a button of steatite; flat and pencil-like whetstones; a button, peg and idol, and two fragments of a horn or bone handle; plaques and disks of ivory decorated in a Mycenaean style with rosettes and a net pattern; terracotta beads, sling pellets, and loom weights both pyramidal and flattened piriform in shape.

52 Debris heaped up by the earthquake that destroyed Troy VI: at left, east wall of House VI E; at extreme right, Section 3 of fortification wall; in centre, stones fallen from one side or the other. The large jars belong to period VIIa when the floor level was even with the rims of the jars.

53 House VI F cleared to level of floor: two rows of five stone-bases for columns divide the building into three aisles – startlingly anticipating the plan of the much later basilica; two additional column bases in the longitudinal axis of the house may be earlier or later than the others.

54 Deep offset in east foundation of House VI F, a feature also common in contemporary Mycenaean architecture.

55 Western corner of House VI M, as it was uncovered by Dörpfeld in 1893; walls of Troy VIIa and VIIb at left.

56 Mycenaean pottery from the layer of Troy VI is illustrated by two high-stemmed drinking cups of the *kylix* shape, a deep two-handled *alabastron*, and a tall stirrup vase. Grey Minyan Ware is represented by a globular stirrup vase, modelled after a Mycenaean shape, and by a large *krater* which was used as a cinerary urn in the cemetery: it had been covered by a flattish bowl (which had lost its stem and served well for a lid).

57 Handles of pots were often made in the form of animal heads. The horse seems to have been the favourite type, no doubt reflecting the tradition of Trojan supremacy in horse-raising. The two heads at the top of the Plate are clearly equine, as are probably also the two outer ones of the second row. Rams and dogs may be represented by the other heads.

58 Jars in Grey Minyan Ware still *in situ* where they had been used as cinerary urns to hold ashes and burned bones of adults and children whose remains were cremated in the Late period of Troy VI.

59 Great mass of squared blocks hurled down by an earthquake from the upper part of the fortification wall of Troy VI on the eastern side of the stronghold.

60 Row of small houses of Troy VII in Squares J 6–7 which were built up against the eastern fortification wall: the latter must consequently have been reconstructed after the earthquake. At right, east wall of House VI E and, beyond it, projecting angle of House VI F. From north.

61 House VII gamma contained at least nine large storage jars which had been sunk deep below the floor and covered with sturdy stone lids; one could therefore walk freely about the floor.

62 Houses of Troy VII (at right) were built against south fortification wall in Squares F-G 9; here too the wall had been reconstructed to the height required. From west.

63 House VII theta of Troy VIIa: six capacious *pithoi* were set deep beneath the floor. One stone lid is still in place over a jar.

64 Miscellaneous objects found in layer of Troy VIIa. They include a steatite mould with many matrices for making ear-rings and beads of gold or silver (both sides are shown); bone peg; bronze arrowhead, perhaps used by an invading Achaean in the attack on Troy; long narrow whet-stone almost rectangular in section; conical button of steatite; button-shaped casting of lead; segmented pin or ornament of ivory or bone.

65 Typical wall of a house of Troy VIIb with a course of irregular ortho-state blocks at ground level.

66 Some objects recovered in deposits of Troy VIIb. Bronze awl tapering to a point and fitted with a bone handle; whetstones of cylindrical shape; conical button of steatite, probably Mycenaean; barbed javelin point with shank for attaching to shaft. The arrowhead (centre) found in the same layer is probably an intruder from a much later period. Figurine of terracotta notable for its crudity, a piece unique at Troy and not closely matched elsewhere.

67 Four characteristic pots of Knobbed Ware: two shallow two-handled cups, one with the handles flattened on top, the other (part only) decorated with a band of stamped circles, each enclosing a dot; a small cup with large handle, decorated with miniature knobs; a huge cup-shaped vessel with one small vertical handle and three large knobs projecting from the side.

Index

Roman numerals denote settlement levels (cf. Chronological Table, p. 174)

Achilles, 15, 18, 21
Aegean, 37
Aeneas, 14
Agamemnon, 14, 18, 163
Agricultural products of Troad at time of Troy II, 88
Aischylos, 21
Ajax, 14, 18
Alexander, see Paris
Alexandria, 162
Amulets: I, 47, 50
Anatolia, 37, 58, 92, 96, 139
Andromache, 14
Angel, J. Lawrence, 143
Animal figurines: III, 95, 98; V, 107
Animal bones: I, 49; II, 71; III, 94; IV, 102; V, 107; VI (first appearance of the horse), 113
Animal-head handles: VI, 140
Antenor, 17
Apollo, 14, 16
Apse, in house of Troy I, 47
Arrowheads of flint: I, 51
Artemis, 14
Asia Minor, 21, 41, 57, 146
Athena, 14
Athos, Mount, 21
Atreus, 17
Awls and pins of bone: I, 47, 51; II, 94

Babaköy, 57f., 85
Bakery or cookshop: VIIa, 154
Balikesir, 58, 85
Balkans, the, 146
Balli Dagh, 23f., 172
Basilica-style house: VI, 136
Battle-axes of stone: I, 51; II (Treasure L), 76f.
Beads, of paste and terracotta: VI, 133; of stone: I, 50
Beans, remains of: II, 71
Berbati, abandonment of, 163
Bessarabia, 77, 86
Bittel, Dr Kurt, 169
Black Sea, 146
Boeotia, 93
Boghaz-köy, 143
Bone objects: I, awls and pins, 47, 51, knife blades, 51; II, 84; III, awls and pins, flat idols, tubes, diadems, 94; IV, 102; V, 107
Bronze, first general use of: V, 78
Bronze or copper, objects of: I, 49ff., fish-hook, 51; II, vessels, daggers, spears, chisels, knives, arrowheads, flat celts, saw, 75, 77f.; III, knife blade, needles, pins, 92f.; IV, pins, needle, awl, figurines or razors, 102; V, chisel, knife; pins, wire, 107; VI, slender knives, 112,

VIIb 2, implements and weapons of new types, 168

Brush-handles of terracotta: II, III, and IV, 96

Bunarbashi, 23

Burials: I, of infants, 48, 57; II, of adult and children, 85; V, of infant, 110; VI, cremation burials, 142f.

'Burnt City' of Schliemann (Troy IIg), 28, 68f., 81

'Burnt layer' of Schliemann (Troy IIg), 74

Buttons, *see* Whorls

Calvert, Frank, 24f.

Castor, 14, 17

Catalogue of Ships, 163

Celts, of copper or bronze: II, 78; of stone: I, 51

Central Anatolia, 37f., 58, 92

Chronology of successive settlements at Troy, 173f.

Cilicia, 37, 88

Cincinnati Archaeological Expedition, 11f., 25, 30, 57, 59, 69, 79, 84ff., 91f., 95, 101, 105, 112f., 116f., 126, 130, 134, 142, 144, 147, 150, 156f., 159, 173

Cinerary urns: VI, 142f.

Cistern or well: VI, 119

Clytemnestra, 21

Colonnade, 148

Column bases of stone: II, 64; VI, 127f., 129f., 135f.

Copper or bronze, first appearance of, 41; objects of, *see* Bronze or Copper

Council Chamber of Roman times, 153

Court in front of *Megaron*: II, 63f., 68

Cremation: VI, 142f.

Crete, 35

Crystal, lion heads made of: II, 77; pommels of, 77; segments of, 76f.

Cyclades, relations with, and objects imported from, 37, 57f., 86, 88, 94

Cyclopean-style masonry: VI, 134

Cyprus, 139

Daggers of bronze or copper: II, 77

Danube valley, 169

Dardanelles, 21, 40, 58

'Dardanian Gate', 15

Decorative art: II, 83

Deiphobos, 13, 14, 18

Depas amphikypellon: II, 81; III, 97; IV, 104; widespread diffusion through neighbouring regions, 87

Destruction of Troy: I, 48f.; II, 69f., 89; III, 99; IV, 105; V, 110; VI, 143f.; VIIa, 153, 161ff.; VIIb 1, 167; VIIb 2, 172

Diadems of gold: II, 74ff.; of horn: III, 94, 97

Diomedes, 14, 17

Dorian Invasion, 162f.

Dörpfeld, Wilhelm, 11, 25, 28, 30f., 36, 43, 59, 62f., 66, 67, 71, 85, 91, 116, 118ff., 121, 123, 125ff., 128ff., 134, 136f., 138, 142, 144f., 147f., 150, 168

Douris, of Samos, 163

Dowel-holes: VI, 131f.

Drain under roadway: VIIa, 149f.

Ear ornaments of gold: II, 75f.

Early Bronze Age in the Aegean, 31, 39, 41

Earthquake: VI, 144, 147, 149

East Gateway: VI, 120, 143, 147f.; VIIa, 147f., VIIb 1, 166; VIIb 2, 167
East Tower: VI, 121
Egypt, 35, 145
Electrum: II, bracelets of, 76; goblet of, 75; pin of, 76
Ephoros of Kyme, 163
Epithets in the epics applied to Ilios and Troy, 16f.; applied to Trojans, 17f.
Eratosthenes, 162
Erdek, 58
Eutresis, knife from, 93; deep stratified deposit at, 173
Evans, Sir Arthur, 31

Face pots: I, 56; II, 82; III, 97; IV, 104
Figurines (or razors) of copper: IV, 102
Food, evidence for: I, 49; II, 71; III, 94f.; IV, 101f.; V, 107; VI, place for cooking, 137f.; VIIa, bakery or cookshop, 154
Fortification walls: I, 43ff.; II, 60ff., 68, 83; III, 91; IV, 100; V, 105; VI, 115–24; VIIa, repaired after earthquake, 144, 147ff., east wall extended, 148; VIIb 1, 165f.; VIIb 2, 167
France, southern: existence of stelae with reliefs resembling those of Troy I, 56
Furumark, Arne, classification and chronology of Mycenaean pottery, 137, 142, 159f., 160, 163

Gallipoli Peninsula, 22
Gateways: I, 44f.; II, 60f., 62f., 67; VI, 115 (plan), 117f., 118 (plan), 119, 120, 121f., 123f., 139
Gejvall, Nils-Gustaf, 94

Gla, destruction of, 163
Gold: abundant in Troy II, 74ff.; objects of, in 'Great Treasure': bracelets, 75; coils, probably hair-fasteners, 74f.; cups, 79; diadems, 75; double sauceboat, 74, 79; ear ornaments and ear-rings, 74f.; other jewellery, 74ff.
Götze, Alfred, 84, 156
Graves: I, 48, 57; II, 85; V, 110; VI, cremation burials, 142f.
'Great Tower' mentioned in *Iliad*, 14
'Great Treasure' found by Schliemann: II, 74, 79, 173
Greece, 35, 38, 58, 141
Greek mainland, 37, 88, 140, 145
Grey Minyan Ware (*see also* Minyan Ware), 140f., 145, 160, 165–72
Grey Polished Ware: II, 81, 140
Grote, George, 23

Hahn, G. von, 23
Hair fasteners, coils of gold: II, 76
Hammer-axes: I, 51; II (Treasure L), 76f.
Hearths: I, 47ff.; II, 66; III, 92; IV, 101 (Fig. 24); V, 106; VI, 132, 137
Hector, 13, 15, 17
Hecuba, 14, 21
Helen, 13, 18
Hellespont, 21, 171
Hera, 15
Hippasos, 17
Hissarlik, 21, 23, 24, 32, 111, 173; mound formed by layers of accumulated deposit, 27f.
Hittites, 37, 143
Homer, 19

Horn of deer: III, carved to represent human head, 94; diadems of, with incised decoration, 94, 97

Horse, first appearance of: VI, 113

'House of the City King': II, 69, 74

Houses in citadel: I, 46ff.; phases IIf and IIg, 68f.; III, 91f.; IV, 100f.; V, 105f.; VI, House 630, 126; Houses VI A, 29, 126f., 132; VI B, 126f., 132; VI C, 126, 127ff., 130f., 132; VI D, 126; VI E, 129, 131, 133f., 144; VI F, 129, 131, 134ff., 152; VI G, 126, 129f., 132, 152; VI M, 137f., 152; VI D, H, J, K, L, N, O, P, Q, 126; Pillar House, 131ff.; Troy VIIa: 150, 153f., 161, House 731, 154; Troy VIIb 1, 165ff.; Troy VIIb 2, 167f.

Human bones: I, 48, 57; II, 84f.; IV, 105; V, 110; VI, 142f.; VIIa, 161

Human figure, scratched on sherd: II, 83f.

Hungary, possible connection with Troy, 169ff.

Hyperenor, 17

Ida, Mount, 15

Idols of bone, shell, and stone: 445 examples belonging to Early Bronze Age, found by Schliemann, indicate continuity of culture through that period, 84; I, 47, 57; II, 84; III, 93f.; IV, 102

Iliad, 13, 15f., 17f., 19, 23, 81

Ilion, 16, 23, 32

Ilios, 16f.

Imbros, 21

Imported pottery: I and II, 86; VI, Matt-painted, 141; Mycenaean wares, 29, 141f.; VIIa, 159f.; VIIb, 173

Incised decoration on pottery: I, 54; II, 82; IV, 102; V, 109

Ivory, use of, in late phases of Troy VI, 112

Jewellery: II, 74ff.

Karo, Georg, 27

Knife blade of bone: I, 51

Knives of bronze or copper: I and II, 78; III, 93; IV, 102; V, 107; VI, 112

Knobbed Ware: VIIb, 165, 169ff.

Knossos, 19, 36

Kum Tepe, 40f., 89

Kusura, 57

Lamb, Winifred, 58

Late Bronze Age, 31

Lead, strip of: V, 107

Lentils, remains of: II, 71

Lerna, 173

Leto, 14

Linear B script, 19, 35

Lion heads, *see* crystal

Loom: II, 71f.

Loom weights of terracotta: I, 49; II, 72f.; V, 107; VI, new types, 112, 133; VIIa, 138

Lustre Ware, red and black: I and II, 81

Lydia, 89

Macedonia, 58

Maclaren, Charles, 23

Marble, amulets of: I, 50; figurines of, resembling Cycladic types: I, 47, 57; II, 84; III, 93f.; IV, 102

Marne, relief sculpture from, resembling stele from Troy, 56

Matting on floor, traces of: I, 47

Matt-painted Ware: VI, 141

Megaron type of house: I, 48; II, 59, 65ff., 68f., 71, 83; VI, 126ff., 132

Menelaus, 14f.

Menhirs in Anatolia and Cyprus, monolithic pillars resembling: VI, 139

Mesopotamia, records on clay tablets, 35

Middle Bronze Age, corresponding to early stages of Troy VI, 31

Millstones, or querns: I, 47; II, 71; VI or VIIa, 138; VIIa, 153

Minyan Ware: distinctive repertory of shapes, 140, 145; theories concerning origin, 141; fired under reducing conditions in kiln, 141; in late phases of Troy VI, used for making some pots of characteristic Mycenaean shapes, 141

Monolithic pillars flanking gateways: VI, 138f.

Moulds of stone and terracotta for daggers: I, 50f.; II, 77f.

Mycenae, 21, 29, 30, 36, 66, 134, 163, 173

Mycenaean pottery, Furumark's chronology, 159f.

Mycenaean pottery of III A and III B styles found in cremation cemetery: VI, 142f.

Mycenaean pottery styles, sequence of, in strata of Troy VI, 141

Necklace of pierced bird bones: I, 50

Needles of copper: I, 50; III, 92f.

Nestor, 18

New stock, arrival of: brings an end to Troy V, 111ff.; contemporary with Middle Helladic invasion of Greek mainland, 145; probably corresponds with first arrival of Greek stock on other side of Aegean, 145f.; later movement, in VIIb 2, from across the Hellespont, 171

Nilsson, Martin P., 19

Northeast Gate: VI, 119f.

Northeast Tower: VI, 117ff.

Northeast Trench of Schliemann, 120, 127

North-South Trench of Schliemann, 43, 46, 64

Obsidian: II, 86; III, 93; IV, 102

Odysseus, 14, 18

Odyssey, 13, 16, 18, 19

Offsets in walls: VI, 111, 116, 120, 121, 122, 123, 134, 138

Ornaments worn by women: I, 47, 50

Orthostate blocks, distinctive feature in buildings of VIIb 2, 165

Ovens of domed type: IV, 101; V, 106f.; VI, 132

Pactolus, 89

Page, Professor Denys, 19f.

Palace in Homeric Troy, 13

Palace style of decoration on pottery, 137

Panthous, 18

Paris, 13, 15

Parry, Milman, 19

Party walls: III, 92; IV, 100; VIIa, 151, 153; VIIb 1 and 2, 167

Paste, beads of: VI, 133

Index

Patroclus, 15, 18

Pellets of stone: I, 51; of terracotta, VI, 133

Peloponnesos, 141

Phrygia, 89

Pillar cult (?) in Tower VI i, 139

Pillar House: VI, 131f., 152

Pithoi, or storage jars: VI, 130, 138; VIIa, 154ff.

Plastic ornament on pottery: I, 52f.; II, 82; III, 98; IV, 104; V, 109

Plaza: VIIa, 152

Poliochni in Lemnos, 58

Pollux, 14

Pommels of crystals: II, 77; of stone: VI, 112

Potter's wheel, introduction of, in Troy IIb, 81

Pottery:

  General characteristics, decoration, shapes, wares: I, 52ff.; II, 79ff.; III, 96ff.; IV, 103f.; V, 108f.; VI, 112f., 140ff.; VIIa, 156ff.; VIIb 1, 165, 167; VIIb 2, 169ff.

  Hand-made wares in Troy I and early II, 52, 81

  Introduction of potter's wheel in Troy IIb, 81

  Monochrome character of pottery of Trojan Early Bronze Age, 82

  New types of wares and shapes replace old at beginning of Troy VI, 111, 112f.

  Some specific wares: Grey and Black Polished, II, 81; Knobbed Ware, VIIb, 2, 165, 168, 169ff.; Lustre Ware, I and II, 81; Matt-painted Ware, VI, 141f.; Minyan Ware, VI, 140f., 145; VIIa, 157, 160; VIIb 1, 165, 167; VIIb 2, 169; Mycenaean Ware, VI, 141f.; VIIa, 159; VIIb 1, 165, 167, 171; VIIb 2, 171; Tan Ware, VIIa, 157f.; VIIb 1, 165, 167; VIIb 2, 169

Priam, King, 13, 15, 16, 18, 19, 162

Prosymna, 163

Protesilaos, 22, 58

Pylos, 19, 36, 66, 134, 163

Quadrupeds, of terracotta: III, 95, 98; V, 107

Querns, or millstones: I, 47; II, 71; VI, 138f.; VIIa, 153

Red Cross bowls: IV, 104; V, 109

Relations of Troy with other regions: in general, 37f.; I, 57f.; II, 86ff.; III, 93f.; VI, 141f., 144; VIIa, 159; VIIb, 169f.

Religious side of life at Troy: I, 56f.; II, 84; III, 94; VI, 138f.

Russia, (?) invaders from, 146

Sanctuary (?) outside Gate VI T, 139

Sauceboat, double, of gold: II, 74, 79, 86

'Scaean Gate', 14

Scamander, 21, 23, 40, 172

Schliemann, Heinrich, 11, 24, 25, 26, 27, 28, 29, 43, 46, 57, 59, 62, 64, 66, 67, 68f., 70f., 74, 78f., 81, 84, 85f., 88f., 91f., 94f., 99, 113, 120, 121, 126f., 130, 168, 173

Schliemann Collection, 36, 77, 79, 84, 92, 94, 102, 157

Schmidt, Hubert, 36, 75, 79, 156f., 165, 170
Sculpture in relief, on stele: I, 54ff.
Semple, Professor W. T., 25
Sesklo, 57
Shrine (?) inside Tower VI i, 139
Silver: abundant in Troy II, 74; objects of, from 'Great Treasure', 75; objects of, from Treasure D, 76
Skeletal remains, human: I, 48, 57; II, 84f.; IV, 105; V, 110; VI, 142f.; VIIa, 161
Soma, 57f., 85
South Gate: VI, 121, 143, 149; VIIa, 149; VIIb 1, 166f.; VIIb 2, 167
South Tower: VI, 121f., 138f.
Southeast Trench of Schliemann, 129f.
Southwest Gate: VI, 123
Spearheads of copper or bronze: II, 77
Spindle of bone, found by Dörpfeld: II, 71
Spindle whorls, *see* Whorls
Spinning: II, 71; VI, 133
Spit rests: I, 49
Stag, crude sketch of, incised on a lid: IV, 102
Stairways in houses: VI, 130, 136, 138
Stiletto, mould for: II, 77f.
Stone:
Miscellaneous objects of: I, 50f.; II, 76f.; III, 93f.; IV, 102f.; V, 107; VI, 112
Specific objects of: amulets, I, 50; arrowheads, I, 51; beads, I, 50; celts, I, 51; figurines or idols, I, 47, 57; II, 84; III, 93f.; IV, 102; hammer-axes, I, 51; II, 76f.; pellets, I, 51; polishers, I, 47; sculptured stele, I, 54ff.; vessels,

I, 49; whetstones, I, 47; II, 219 (Pl. 26); V, 220 (Pl. 36); VI, new types, 112
Storage jars, *see* pithoi
Strabo, 89
Stratification: I, 41f.; II, 59f.; III, 91; IV, 99; V, 105; VI, 113f.; VIIa, 147, 160, 165; VIIb 1, 165; VIIb 2, 165
Streets: III, 92; IV, 100; VI, 121, 124, 129; VIIa, 149; VIIb 1, 167; VIIb 2, 167f.
Syria, 35, 87, 88, 145
Syros, 37

Tables of offerings, of stone: I, 56f.
Tankard of silver, in which jewellery of 'Great Treasure' was found: II, 75
Temple of Athena, 113, 124
Tenedos, 21
Terracotta:
Miscellaneous objects of: I, 49, 57; II, 71f.; III, 95f.; IV, 102f.; V, 107f.; VI, 112, 133; VIIa, 138; VIIb 2, 168f.
Specific objects of: beads, VI, 133; brush-handles, II, III, and IV, 96; figurines, I, 57; VIIb 2, 168f.; loom weights, I, 49; II, 72f.; V, 107; VI, 112, 133; VIIa, 138; moulds for casting weapons, I, 5cf.; II, 77f.; pellets, VI, 133; quadrupeds, III, 95, 98; V, 107; whorls or buttons, I, 49; II, 71, 88; III, 95f.; IV, 102; V, 108; VI, 112
Textiles: II, 72, 88; (?) workshop of: VI, 133

Index

Thebes in Boeotia, palace at, 163

Thermi in Lesbos, 58

Thrace, 58, 170

Thrasymedes, 17

Timber produced in the Troad, 88

Tiryns, 29, 30, 36, 66, 163

Towers in fortification walls: I, 44; II, 60f., 62; VI, 119ff., 121, 122, 129, 138, 148, 149f.

Trade in the time of Troy II, 87

Trapezoidal plans of houses: VI, 129, 133, 134

'Treasures' found by Schliemann: 69, 74; the 'Great Treasure' (A), 74f.; Treasure D, 76; Treasure L, 76f.; Treasure M, 71

Trojan War, historical basis for, 20

Troy of the Homeric poems, 13ff.

Troy, the archaeological, 21ff.

Troy I, 39–58; Troy II, 59–90; Troy III, 91–9; Troy IV, 99–105; Troy V, 105–10; Troy VI, 111–46; Troy VIIa, 147–64; Troy VIIb 1, 165–7; Troy VIIb 2, 167–72

Tydeus, 17

Ventris, Michael, 19, 35

Vetch, remains of: II, 71; VIIa, 154

Walls of houses: usually built of crude brick laid on a stone socle, 32; III, built entirely of stone, 91f.; VIIa, largely built with squared blocks dislodged by earthquake from walls and houses of Troy VI, 149f., 154; VIIb 2, with small orthostate blocks set in the lowest course, 168

Weapons: I, mainly of stone, 50f.; II, stone, copper, and bronze, 76ff.; VIIb 2, bronze, of new types, 168

Well, or cistern, inside Northeast Tower: VI, 119; in paved court: VI and VIIa, 152

Western Gateway: VI, 123f.

Wheat, remains of: II, 71; VIIa, 154

Whetstones: I, 47, 51; II, 219 (Pl. 26); V, 220 (Pl. 36); VI, new types, 112

Whorls or buttons of terracotta: I, 49f.; II, 71f., 88; III, 95; IV, 102f.; V, 108; VI, 112, 133

Women, status of, in Troy II, 76

Wool, production of, in the Troad: I, 49f.; II, 71, 88

Yortan, 57f.; 85

Zygouries, 163